DELIGHTFUL ENCOUNTERS

WITH

GOD'S LITTLE CREATURES

TRUE STORIES OF FAITH, HOPE AND INSPIRATION

S. Jenny Boyer

S. JENNY BOYER

ILLUSTRATED BY GAY PETRLIK

Become aware of the little creatures!

ISBN 13: 978-1-61244-315-7
Library of Congress Control Number: 2014917029

Printed in the United States of America

Published by Halo Publishing International
1100 NW Loop 410
Suite 700 - 176
San Antonio, Texas 78213
Toll Free 1-877-705-9647
www.halopublishing.com
www.holapublishing.com
e-mail: contact@halopublishing.com

IN MEMORY OF MY BELOVED SISTER
GAY PETRLIK

ACKNOWLEDGMENTS

Sharing my stories is a privilege. The following people helped make this book possible.

My dear friend and editor, Maritta Perry Grau, whose touch to my stories only made them better.

Peter Perez II, my personal photographer.

Friends who were willing to listen to or read my words and share their opinions of my stories.

My sister, Gay, who drew my words.

My daughters, Sarah, Laura, and Amanda, and my stepdaughter, Michelle, who gave me constant encouragement to follow my dream.

My husband, Jim, who makes sure I have the quiet times I need to gather my thoughts and write them down.

CONTENTS

A little creature will touch your life soon,
Be ready to be blessed. SJB

LONESOME DOVE

A COUPLE NO MORE

She actually became a widow a few years ago on a glorious, bright day of summer when only the finest things of life are expected to happen. They were so content as a couple, always flying together, at times soaring high into the sky, letting the wind and their wings take them to heights most earthbound creatures never experience. At other times, they perched side by side on the branches of the towering trees in our yard, seemingly positioned in those particular locations just for their pleasure. They frequently called to each other, full of spirit and full of hope. They had no real worries, having a warm home, loving family and friends, and plenty to eat and drink. Life was so good.

Up and down they swooped, the sun warm on their silver-tinted feathers. They had been together for at least three years. Some close friends called them the perfect match. They enjoyed the same things, communicated well, and had the same ideals about home and family. They were not just a couple of doves, they were a dove couple, mating for life.

Then, in the time it took an eye to blink, a flicker of an eyelid, life as she knew it was gone. She knew when she heard the awful thudding sound, then silence, that things were not good. Showing off one of his flying acrobatic tricks that he took such pleasure in performing for her, he had unwittingly flown head first into a sliding glass door that was pretending to be an opening to another world. His still, small body did not move as he lay on the porch beneath the watching, unrepentant door.

She didn't know what to do to help him. He usually took charge in times of crisis. Doing the only thing she could think of, she flew swiftly to his side and pushed on his quiet breast with her shaking beak. He made no response, his eyes stayed closed, and his neck was tilted at a funny angle. She walked unsteadily around him several times, calling over and over to him in the cooing sounds that she knew he loved, but he did not get up to fly away with her. He was far too quiet, far too still.

Friends passing by, flying high in the sky, not realizing her dilemma, were calling for them to come along. The sun was setting, and it was time to fly to their home for the night. But how does one leave a mate she is supposed to be with her entire life? How does one say a final goodbye on a lonely, impersonal cement porch to all her hopes and dreams when there has been no warning, no time to prepare for this great unwanted life change?

She looked at him with eyes filled with all the love in her heart. She knew she had to go, and accept leaving him behind. By staying on the porch so long, she was drawing unwanted attention to them and it was no longer safe. There was no other choice. There was no choice at all.

When she returned to the porch early the next day, it was empty. Her lover was no longer there. She called to him softly anyway, but the surrounding silence screamed at her. Any remaining hope that he had somehow miraculously survived his accident left her then. It was not just a bad dream, it was the worst of nightmares and it belonged to her. She knew he was gone forever, but how was she supposed to go on without him? No sane answer came to her.

The days passed. She flew automatically where she was supposed to go. She ate a few of the seeds that fell to the ground, eating enough at least to keep her going, as other birds ate energetically from the high birdfeeders. Often she called out to him as she mourned her loss, but no longer did she really expect an answer. Friends tried to help her find ways to occupy her time. They did not leave her alone for long, but nothing was the same. "Tedious" was often the term she used when thinking of how her day had been.

O God, at times like these, why does the sun continue to come up each morning? Why do the hours themselves keep passing? There are so many unanswered questions. Help us, O God, to understand the down-times of our lives, as well as to treasure the good-times.

Years passed, and she still visited the same places they had discovered together. She would fly miles and miles in the spring to get to their favorite warm weather home, and later in the fall she would go in another direction to a milder climate where she would stay during the approaching winter months.

Everyone thought she was doing well since her loss. She did what had to be done, but she was so lonely. Of course, there were still her faithful friends, but there was no one special to share her dreams. No one knew if she was late returning home at night. No one called cheerfully to her just to see if her day was going well. She still missed him so much.

Though she had fooled others over the years, and some of those closest to her even thought she was happy, she had not fooled herself. She knew her true identity. She was made of a broken heart and unshed tears. She knew what they called other dove widows behind their backs: lonesome doves.

It was what she had become, A Lonesome Dove. It was her fate, not her choice.

O God, there are people in this world who make us believe they are happy when they are really very sad. Often they continue to bring joy to others while still grieving themselves, sometimes for years. Allow us to see them as they truly are, and to help them find Your peace while on this earth.

SPARKEY

JENNY, GAY, AND MIKE

FALL THROUGH THE ICE

Sparkey was my first dog, and she was also my first best friend. She came into my life when the years, just like the Milky Way in the night sky above my house, all stretched ahead with alluring promise and without an end in sight. Sparkey was a gentle, black and white, medium-sized spaniel that we always referred to as our "Bird Dog." In her later years, the birds actually sat on her wide back as she wandered around our yard, no longer able to see well from clouded eyes, but capable of negotiating her way safely within the familiar boundary of our property. That birds would be so friendly to her only seemed natural to me at the time; after all, she was a "Bird Dog."

Sparkey had many adventures, as all dogs do, but one of my most vivid memories of her took place right across the street from where we lived. Our home was directly opposite a lovely man-made lake constructed in the 1930s at the end of a large public park running the length of several blocks through our town. At that time the lake was part of the western boundary that divided the city cousins and country cousins.

Sparkey spent endless hours, in all seasons of the year, slowly meandering around the graveled—later blacktopped—path that circled the lake, and I am sure she considered it her own personal sanctuary. However, she willingly shared it with all who stumbled across her little oasis, and that included people of all sizes and shapes, as well as a multitude of other animals, many of whom were just passing through.

She daily greeted the ever-changing population of wild ducks, whom she considered to be agreeable friends. They left her alone, and she did likewise. She had fewer positive feelings about the transient geese population. On occasion, she had to speed up her walk to prevent a pecking attack from the pesky geese that would silently await her approach. They always acted as though they did not see her coming along her path. Then suddenly, as a group, the geese would begin to chase her, flapping their huge white wings and hissing madly, hoping to make her reverse her planned direction. Sparkey just quickened her steady pace forward, and after a while the frenzy died down, the geese becoming bored with their own useless taunting. They were never her friends, but she tolerated them and put up with their frequent temper tantrums. They were who they were.

In the winter, ice skating was a seasonal highlight for the kids like us, lucky enough to live on one of the streets surrounding the park and the lake so appreciated by Sparkey. Once the weather turned consistently cold, and the ice covered the lake from one side to the other for several days, the city officials would arrive with special ice measuring tools. They checked to see if the ice was thick enough to hold the many people who would find their way there once the official "OK" to skate was given. My sister, brother, and I wanted the honor of being the first to make our mark on the pristine, unscratched, glassy surface of the lake. By taking turns watching for the anticipated ice testing to occur, we were almost always among the earliest of the neighborhood kids to grab our skates and tattoo the mirrored skin of the ice. It also didn't hurt our chances that the official sign allowing skating was always put up directly opposite our house.

We often tried to hurry the ice thickness testing process by checking out the ice ourselves. If we thought it was ready, we would call City Hall. Believe it or not, the officials often responded to our calls asking for an ice assessment. I think that kind of response would be unheard of today. There are way too many channels to go through, and rules to follow, not necessarily wrong, but they have a tendency to slow down quick answers to simple requests.

One day, my brother and sister and I were doing our self-appointed job of testing the ice for its skating potential. This was especially crucial, since there had been no ice skating yet that year. Sitting on the low cement pier at one side of the lake, we pressed our booted feet down hard on the ice. We heard the well-known, painful crackling sounds that indicated our wait for ice skating to begin was not yet over.

We were about to head home, when we heard a familiar barking coming from near the direction of the stone fountain at the center of the lake. Slipping and sliding towards us on the ice, seemingly without a care in the world, was Sparkey. We all looked at her and then at each other. We had just concluded that the ice was too thin to support any significant weight, and we instinctively knew Sparkey's innocent walk on deceptively frozen water was not going to end well. We felt helpless, because there was nothing we could do to change her fate.

Step by step, she proceeded toward us. She had probably cut short her morning walk around the lake when she heard our laughter and voices as we tested the ice. We called to her gently, encouraging her to keep coming toward us since by this time she was already past the fountain, more than halfway across the lake.

Then, right before our eyes, Sparkey vanished! She fell

through the ice into the frigid, dark water below. By now we were all screaming in voices that should have shattered all the icicles hanging from the trees surrounding the lake and beyond. My sister ran back across the street, yelling hysterically for our parents to help us. Thank goodness, our dad was home from work, having his lunch. My brother and I examined the ice in front of us, desperate for any sign of Sparkey, but it was no use. The ice pieces had simply come back together where Sparkey had fallen through, and there was no opening for her to find a way back onto the ice from the water.

The lake water was deep and unclear, and the bottom an unknown, scary place. We had been told endless times by our parents, even though we could all swim well, never to go into the deeper water in the middle of the lake for any reason. We were also forbidden to walk out on the ice until it had been officially approved for skating.

In response to my sister's hysterical explanation of our problem, my parents came running across the street to the pier. My dad had grabbed some bricks from around the garden on his way. He tried throwing them onto the ice to create a hole for Sparkey to come back to the surface and get some air. The bricks hardly dented the surface of the ice, except where it was thinner right beside the pier where we were all standing. By now we were all crying and yelling Sparkey's name over and over, but to no avail. There was no sign of Sparkey. Our beloved dog was gone.

Looking so very sad, my parents and my younger siblings returned to our house across the street. I refused to leave the lake where my best friend had disappeared; however, I was made to promise not to venture out on the ice to look for my precious dog. I was cold, and feeling very alone.

Soon my brother and sister came back and quietly sat at my side on the steps of the pier. Silent tears were streaming down all of our faces. We all really loved that dog, and we were inconsolable. We had lost an adored pet, and it had happened right before our eyes.

After a while, we heard a new odd crackling sound from the direction of the ice. We looked at each other. What was going on? Now, as an adult, I truly believe that there have been many wonderful miracles in my life. However, the first miracle I remember was the head of Sparkey emerging through the broken ice beside the end of the pier. She paddled quickly to the shallow water by the edge of the lake, which was not frozen solid because of the bricks my dad had thrown on it. Together, while laughing and shouting with pure joy, we were able to pull her out of the water. We wrapped her in the old torn blankets that were part of the rescue paraphernalia my mother had snatched earlier, and carried Sparkey back across the street to our home and our amazed parents.

I remember we all rubbed her with towels, and my mother gave her a warm water-milk mixture to drink. Sparkey looked at us like she couldn't understand why she was getting all this attention, but she appreciated being the center of our lives on this day. None of us wanted to leave her side. Sparkey was fine. We didn't even need to take her to the vet.

Our family discussed many times over the years how Sparkey survived under the ice for well over one-half an hour. The theory most of us believe is that since the ice was not yet frozen solid, uneven freezing had allowed air pockets to form under the ice surface, providing Sparkey with essential large bubbles of air to breathe as she made her way to the side of the lake. She must have paddled from bubble to bubble towards the sound of our shouting voices as we called to her over and over.

We would never know for sure the answer to our questions regarding her survival, of course, but the best black-and-white Bird Dog in the whole world was back in my arms, and happily she lived with us for many more years.

Was this a God thing? Of course it was! Did I know it at the time? Not really, but I did know that some extraordinary event had occurred in my life. Even without a clear understanding of what had happened, I knew Whom to thank for watching over Sparkey and bringing her safely back to our family.

MUSIC TREE

BREAK OF DAY CONCERTS

I am known to be one of those exasperating people who become instantly awake when my eyes open in the morning, and to make matters worse, I wake up very early. Often I just lie still for a while, listening for the rare sounds of other creatures stirring in God's world that is still covered with a blanket of darkness. It is usually around four a.m., and other than an occasional peeper's lonely call, or a solitary cricket's high chirp that is bringing to a close the summer nightlife in the woods in back of my house, I hear only the distinct, intriguing sound of silence wrapped around my little part of the world. I so appreciate these quiet minutes just before the breaking of dawn, which comes earlier in the warmer months than in any other season, and seems to have a tendency to linger longer before the day begins. For me it is a time of peaceful contemplation and quiet planning for the day ahead.

On the dead-end street in the front of our home, a lonely garbage truck rumbles by. It makes its way quietly, starting, then stopping to swallow whatever meal the neighbors have put in those big blue plastic containers that act as neighborhood sentinels for each home. Then the garbage truck meanders to the next street, eager to start the process all over again, its hunger never satisfied. Later, if I stay still long enough, a newspaper delivery car slows at most homes, an invisible arm pushing today's good and bad news into patiently waiting paper holders. There is no loitering, the driver having long ago mastered the art of slowing a car enough to dispense a paper, yet keeping the forward motion continuous, if slightly jerky.

As this time of fading darkness passes, and it seems to quicken its pace minute by minute, I think of God, the Creator of all things. I begin this new day by inviting Him into my life. I read His Word, and pray, asking for open eyes and open ears so that I don't miss what He wants to show me in the coming day. I pray for His touch on those who do not yet know Him, and healing for so many crying out to Him for comfort.

Thy will be done this day, Father God. Thank you for all those You will bring into my path today, and for all that You have planned for me to do if I am responsive to Your leading.

It is during this time of end of night quiet that I am one of a few privileged early risers to hear a very special sound. A single note, so pure and so hushed that I need to listen intently to be certain I am hearing that softest of sounds. There it is again, that same quiet note repeated. I smile. It is my invitation to today's Break of Day Concert, otherwise known as Morning Birdsong. It is a time a variety of bird choirs from the fields and the woods join in unscripted harmony to greet the new day. Hastily then, as if all the bird alarm clocks are set to go off at exactly the same time, the day's concert unfolds. An enticing blend of chirps, peeps, trills, and whistles begins to fill the air from this unseen orchestra in God's music trees. As I listen, the Birdsong seems to gain momentum, as new participants add their voices to the unique mixture of sound.

This glorious performance is a call for me to check out the status of the painting of the canvas in the eastern skyline by the Master Artist. Today, varying shades of brilliant pink, blue, and gold are splashed in perfect symmetry before my eyes. If I am patient, I will see the bright orange tip of the sun rise above the lightening horizon, dissolving the remaining wisps of night and hiding any lingering stars. Suddenly, the Morning Birdsong I have been listening to fades away into an all encompassing silence, with only an occasional chirp or peep to remind the fortunate listener of what just occurred.

Some of my still unanswered earthly questions include: what happens to the Birdsong at just this moment; in other words, how do all the birds know to cease their singing at the same time? Do these numerous creatures of all shapes, colors, and sizes really sing less after the sun rises, or is it that the awakening of the rest of the world intrudes with a cacophony of sound that simply swallows up the sweet Birdsong into the rest of the day?

Whatever the answers to these questions, it is reassuring to know the Great Conductor of Life will surely have another performance for me tomorrow, if I just make time to be blessed. All are welcome. The performance is free for everyone.

KK

INVISIBLE ONE

For a number of years, we have had a cat whose name is KK. Most of our extended family, including our grown children and grandchildren, have never seen her. We have actually heard them murmuring to each other, questioning why we persist in saying that we have two cats. It just so happens that KK is invisible to most people; that is just her nature.

Her life story, at least as much as is known to me, started on a dark, dreary winter afternoon in January, several years ago. The year's first blizzard was stretching out its arms, wrapping as much of the world as it could in its full fury. Heavy snow and punishing winds swirled together, changing the outside world into a place strangely beautiful, and yet as if by design, extremely menacing at the same time. All familiar outdoor objects of color were now deformed, unrecognizable shapes in shades of black, gray and white. Nothing looked typical. The road could no longer be seen in the front of the house, and the hedges and fences that separated neighbors' yards no longer garlanded the landscape. The deep snow had smoothed out boundaries, making uniformity, not uniqueness, the rule. It was "not fit outside for man nor beast," as the old saying goes.

As the woman stood gazing out the window, mesmerized by the endless undulating motion of the cold white scene before her, she heard a tiny bell-like sound that was very different from the persistent howling wind. On hearing it repeated, she thought it sounded sort of like the peeping of a tiny bird. Looking down at the flowerbox on the top of the window sill, at first all she saw was as expected, a huge mound of snow. However, where the flowerbox nestled closely to the house, she saw a diminutive black animal almost completely covered with pointed ice shards. She thought it must be a mouse trying to find a way get inside the warm house to escape the ravaging storm. Could that peep-like sound have come from that tiny creature? Could anything that small even possibly be alive outside in this freezing weather? She watched intently for a few seconds as the tiny animal clung with determination, and probably the last of its strength, to a small section of bare wood at the edge of the flowerbox, that had somehow been blown free of snow. That animal had absolutely nowhere else it could go.

Known for being extremely kind-hearted, the woman decided there was nothing else to be done but to go and retrieve the tiny animal, whatever it was. The bell-like sound she had heard meant it was alive, and it definitely needed someone's immediate help. Since she was the only one present, she had to act fast. After putting on all the warm clothes she could gather around her body and still be able to move, she stepped out the front door and carefully inched her way down the buried brick steps. She proceeded as fast as she could through 20 inches of snow, finally reaching the inhabited flowerbox. Normally, that distance was just a few yards from the front porch, but today with the blizzard trying its best to stop her, it seemed like it was much further away.

On an ordinary day, when God's creatures could see and hear what was happening in their world, the little animal probably would have heard her coming and would have for sure escaped her touch. However, the wailing of the blizzard and its deep blanket of white successfully muffled the sounds of her boots sinking through the snow's crusty cover. Finally, the woman was able to reach up and grab the motionless animal, and carried it as quickly as possible to her warm house. Back inside, much to the woman's surprise as she tenderly opened her gloved hand and gazed at the little life form, she realized she had rescued a very small, limp, feral kitten.

O God, how can a creature this tiny even be alive in such a howling blizzard? No vets are accessible because of the storm. Please put your healing hand on this precious animal that You brought to this house this day.

Soft cloths saved for polishing family treasures were quickly brought out to wrap the ice-covered animal, now beginning to visibly melt before the woman's eyes. A warm solution of diluted milk was dribbled into the animal's mouth with the end of a tiny spoon left from feeding many grandbabies over the years long past. Caring hands massaged the little body whose chest was hardly moving, and soothing words worked their own magic to restore the life force that seemed to be trying to seep out of the tiny living thing.

Slowly but surely the afternoon slipped into evening, any real separation between the two times of day being difficult to define in the continuing blizzard. The little creature looked as if it was gaining strength before the woman's eyes. As it dried off and warmed up, the little bundle of frozen fur turned into a petite kitten wearing a shaggy black and tan coat, and looked very much like a Tortoiseshell cat. It was really love at first sight between those two, the gentle woman and the lucky kitten. That very night that little creature was adopted into the woman's heart family, the family God had picked out for both of them before time began. The kitten was given the name "Kit Kat," and became the newest sibling to an already much-loved older dog and cat.

Over the next several years, the woman and her furry children all made each other very happy. The new kitten grew into an elfin-like cat, and not surprisingly, was totally absorbed into her new family. Kit Kat's well-honed feral instincts had allowed her to survive a rough young life. Those same wild longings to suddenly escape to places known only to her, and her frequent unannounced times away from home, did not seem to cause serious problems for her family. These habits made her somewhat unusual, but not unacceptable. They knew she had no human clock to help her tell the date and time. Even when she ignored them as they called her given name, they never got really annoyed with her. They had learned that she would return when she was ready, and when she needed a dose of comfort and stability and a good meal.

Interestingly enough, few people outside of the woman's visiting grown children, even knew this second cat existed. Her streak of skittishness never really left her, and humans as a group had never been high on her preference list. We truly thought she believed she could become invisible if the need arose. When anyone visited the house and Kit Kat was inside, she would simply run to one of her numerous hiding places and disappear, seeking protection from prying eyes and poking hands. Once the visitors left and all became quiet again, she would return to snuggle in her favorite place on the sofa next to the woman, the only human she considered worthy of her time and attention.

As day flowed into day, and season after season, some changes occurred in the little family. The older dog and cat went to animal heaven, and it became time for the woman to move to a smaller home, and get some help with her daily care. However, there was one big stumbling block to this major life change: the woman could not take her remaining adored pet with her to the new living quarters that suited her best. Cats, even invisible ones, were not allowed in the level of care she required. What would happen to the precious cat that loved only her? Who, if anyone, would take an invisible cat into their home? The woman refused to budge any further on the matter of moving, until Kit Kat's future was settled to her satisfaction.

*O God, there comes a time in life when You make a decision for us. I know without a doubt that we are supposed to take Kit Kat into our home. The problem is, my husband does not like cats, and we already have one that adopted us for reasons known only to You. Help us work this out, God, as only You are a*ble.

So Kit Kat's life story ended up just as it was planned from the beginning of time. To keep the loving woman's heart from breaking, I volunteered—and my husband finally agreed—to take Kit Kat into our home. Then the woman and the cat could visit each other, since the woman's new home would be much closer to where we lived. All the family members were now in agreement about the upcoming moves, except for Kit Kat. She only knew well one small area of the enormous world, and new things forced on her were scary. She would rather live on her own than take a chance with other humans that were not both certain they even wanted another cat.

Moving day arrived. The woman was taken to her lovely, new, extended-care home, and the terrified cat, who was trying her best to be invisible in a home that was now almost empty, was coerced into her travel box and brought to live with us. It was Thanksgiving week, and already getting very cold outside, especially at night. To ensure that Kit Kat did not run away and freeze to death, we made her a cat cave in our basement. The beautiful, friendly tabby cat we already had was named T, and we shortened our newest boarder's name from Kit Kat to KK, a name that just popped out every time we talked of her.

We did not touch KK again for about five months. All of her wild protective instincts had made a swift return. She found multiple places to hide in our basement, her favorite spots being inside a large pile of uneven, oak boards that my husband had harvested from our yard. Our lives revolved around each other, but the strange cat and the people living in the same house were not involved with each other.

Cat food was given and disappeared without any purring thanks.

The cat box was used and emptied with no meow comments.

The water level in the dish went down and was replenished, with no appreciation, as far as we could tell.

The cat's names, both old and new, were frequently called with no visible response.

The only time KK was reported being seen for any length of time was when the gentle woman visited. She would make her way slowly down the basement steps and settle into a soft chair we had placed for her beside the woodpile. After a while, we would hear murmurings and soft crooning sounds, and even some laughter. But when she called to us, and we went down into the basement to assist the woman back upstairs, there was nothing but her to be seen. These visits came to a sad stop when the woman was no longer strong enough to make the trip to our home.

O God, let the woman be at peace, knowing that her beloved cat has a good home. Let KK not always live her life invisible to all but You and T.

We always left the door to our basement open so KK could join us upstairs if she ever chose to do so. As the months passed, we began to have an occasional flash sighting of the cat we now referred to as "Invisible One," usually caught spying on us from the darkness of the basement steps. However, no cat visitations were made from below, except by our other cat, T.

Winter finally waned, and spring stepped into her rightful place of authority as green colors replaced the browns in our yard, and the fuzzy pussy willows and the bright yellow forsythia set the tone for the beginning of the season of new birth. The crocus popped up in clumps of vibrant purple, white and gold, some materializing in dirty patches of snow remaining on the ground by the fence posts. Birds that we hadn't see since they left for warmer climates over the winter, returned and began harmonizing in our trees right outside our windows. The redbuds, hollies and the tall oaks beckoned to them to nest in their waiting branches. Flowers of all colors arranged themselves in bouquets around our yard, making the view a magnificent picture whose colors and subjects changed on a daily basis.

One day, while sipping my morning coffee on the old oak church bench at the end of our kitchen, I glimpsed a small black and tan head peeking around the corner of the doorway to the basement. Another day soon after, a ball of black fur crept slowly into the kitchen, then darted back down the basement steps. After a week of cautious exploration, KK started to extend her excursions deeper into the kitchen. Finally one day, she came directly to me as I sat quietly on the kitchen bench, and just for an instant, let me touch her head.

Slowly, KK and I got to know each other, and she began to join me on the bench in the morning for some exclusive petting. It was now warm outside, and with the reinforcement of her big brother T, I was able to introduce her to our wonderful backyard. It is a perfect place for cats to roam and explore endlessly. T became her mentor, and KK did not like to stray far from his side. Quickly, she found new places outside in which to hide, and our backyard replaced her basement domain. However, during this time of transition from the basement to outside living, once again no other people ever saw KK. She still had the power to become invisible when she felt the need. When I called her name, there was usually no response until KK decided it was time for her to acknowledge me. Once a feral cat, always a feral cat, I guess.

We fell into an easy family routine. Both cats now lived outside in the warmer months, each enjoying their own private cat house. I provided food and water, and T and KK ate and drank, and personally thanked me with purrs, and rubs on my legs. My husband tried to ignore us all when we were frolicking together.

It was always so easy to love our big orange tabby cat, T. On the other hand, it had been difficult to get close to KK in any way, let alone to love her, and then it had to be on her terms. Along the way, as often happens when least expected, the love between KK and I grew. KK taught me lessons I obviously needed to learn about being patient, and reminded me of the unconditional love and acceptance that all of God's creatures receive from Him, and also need from each other. KK is truly ours now, she is family as long as she wants to stay.

O God, all along you knew that there were more lessons in life I needed to learn, and one way of teaching me was to bring KK into my life. Thank You for asking us to take a chance on her. By doing so, we made a woman very special to us peaceful in her last days, and I found out that it takes time to fall in love with an invisible cat, but it is worth the wait.

HUMMER

LOST BUT NOT ALONE

Our home on a country acre backs up to a charming, wandering wooded area on one side, and a small, proud field just the right size for a vegetable garden on the other. At the dawning of each new day, regardless of the season, we are privileged to view one of God's earthly paintings as it becomes visible before us in the eastern sky. The changing hues and colors on the horizontal canvas often culminate in a wondrous sunrise. As if this is not enough, this event is often accompanied by a birdsong concert, sometimes made up of dozens of performers, at other times featuring a brave, lone, soloist. The blended results of sound and color leave no doubt as to the identity of the artist-conductor.

We are not alone in the audience, though we are hard pressed to find other human participants out and around at this hour of the day. Squirrels, rabbits, birds, mice, and wilder animals like deer and turkeys join us at their will, in appreciation of the early morning experience. Most of the time these creatures are content to stay in our yard, knowing, I guess, that big, noisy, perhaps dangerous humans inhabit the house nearby.

Occasionally, however, one of the animals becomes curious about the garage attached to the end of the house. At least once or twice a year, a bird will decide that she wants to nest in that nice, large dry area, with its high ceiling and many hiding places. It is hard to believe how quickly a pile of sticks and yard debris changes into an elaborate woven nest, and often in exactly the same spot on the top shelf in the back corner of the garage where I store my bee hat. Birds don't usually plan far in advance, so once they decide on a location to nest, their work is intense. The fluttering activity required to accomplish this building feat usually alerts us that our garage is about to be inhabited by a bird couple, soon to become a bird family. We would swiftly become bird grandparents if we did not quickly take action. Our family cat, KK, made the garage an unsafe haven for bird babies, and there is no access to the garage when we are at work during the day as we keep the doors shut and locked. Immediate eviction of the builders' nest prior to laying of their eggs is required for the good of all involved.

At the end of one typical sultry summer day, I slowly meandered around the yard, trying to find a touch of a cool evening breeze. One of our four daughters had checked in by phone, and she was sharing with me her news of the day.

A slight, but rather frantic movement inside the garage caught my eye in the dusky light as I passed by the small, open garage door. Wishing that I had a pair of night vision goggles, as seen in all the action movies these days, I strained to identify the fast-moving object flittering about. At first I thought it might be a summer bat seeking a ready meal from the many insects that are drawn to the heated windows in the garage during the day. However, those fluttering wings I was seeing were not big enough for a bat, and they were too big for a bee. It was too late in the day for it to be a bird building a nest; the tiny sticks that were needed were almost invisible. As I slowly went closer, I could just barely distinguish those wings, so fragile and beating so fast that they could only belong to one type of creature, a hummingbird. This particular tiny, green-cloaked fellow was definitely not trying to build a nest, he was lost and desperately trying to find his way back to the familiarity of his outside habitat. Even though the double garage door for cars and the smaller access door were wide open, his frightened and confused state was causing him to fly erratically without thought or instinct, always flying in the wrong direction from that needed to make his escape.

My animal-lover daughter on the other end of the phone advised me that an immediate rescue of the hummingbird was needed. The tiny bird would tire quickly, using so much energy in his frightened state that he could actually die. She said a quick goodbye and hung up the phone so I could go into my rescue mode. Just what that would be I had no idea, but that is what mothers of all ages are expected by their children to do, come up with a solution to the problem, whatever it is!

Believe it or not, the first thing that came to my mind as I ran inside to enlist in the help of my husband, was to name this little green bird "Hummer." I find it easier to refer to even a casual acquaintance by name, rather than by an impersonal pronoun like he, she, or it. I am sure hundreds of other hummingbird friends are given this same name each year, but this was not the time for great thought or deliberation, as related to naming the faerie-like creature claiming my rapt attention.

I urgently explained to my husband that I needed help to rescue the tiny bird. Just what we should do I still didn't have any idea, since my presence, even though outside the garage, had seemed to upset Hummer even more. After running outside to check out the situation, the first thing my husband suggested was to turn on all the lights outside the garage. As he did this, I continued to watch Hummer's persistent, yet vain attempts to find his way to safety. His efforts to escape were all so futile. He kept flying up to the items stored high near the ceiling of the garage, for some reason avoiding both of the now highly visible, wide-open doorways.

We thought briefly of trying to trap Hummer with an old fishing net, but immediately realized we could unintentionally injure him more than help him, by trying to confine in a web of string such an extremely frightened animal.

Intermittently, Hummer would land for a few seconds on a rope or on one of the wires dangling from the garage ceiling. While he was at rest, with the garage lights now on I could now see his coloring was vastly different from most of the hummingbirds we currently were seeing in our gardens. At this time of year, they were an unusually drab dull brown or muted green color, with very few if any of the special markings seen in pictures of these beautiful birds. Hummer was of the truly dazzling variety, with his scarlet throat edged in pure white under a jet black hood, and a fitted, bright emerald-green coat. His long, pointed black beak was attached to a head which seemed to be on a swivel, as he turned it rapidly from side to side, anxiously seeking a path to escape this strange place, by now certain to feel like a prison.

Right then I could see no good end in sight for Hummer. My only hope was that as darkness continued to deepen, the brightness from the outside lights would guide him to safety. After one last look around and nothing more we could think to do to help this little being, we went back inside the house to wait and to hope for Hummer's getaway.

O God, this little creature is such a beauty. Please watch over him and guide him to safety. We don't know what else to do to try to help him, but You know all things.

A short while later, my husband and I went back outside to check the garage for signs of Hummer's continued presence. We saw no frenzied fluttering of wings, no tiny bird making desperate attempts to return to the endless freedom just beyond the garage doors. We both breathed a sigh of relief, but just to be absolutely sure Hummer had made a clean get away before we turned off the lights and closed up the garage for the night, we decided to check the nooks and crannies in the garage where in his distressed state our little friend could possibly be hiding.

Suddenly, to our great dismay, we saw his small, very still body. My heart seemed to stop my chest for a moment, and then it began to pound erratically. At the back corner of the workbench, on a small shiny flat board, lay Hummer. His wings were twisted as if they were both broken, and at first glance he did not seem to be breathing.

Fearing the worse, and afraid to directly touch him and possibly harm him even more, we gently moved him on his makeshift wooden stretcher to our patio table. We knew he must be severely injured, or totally exhausted, because he did not attempt to stir as we carried him. In fact, I thought Hummer must be dead. No breaths seemed to come from his tiny breast, and his scarlet throat was so very still. I had to put on my glasses to confirm that he indeed was still breathing at all. He was breathing, but barely.

O God, we don't know how to care for a tiny creature like this, especially one that is injured. What should we do now?

My husband remembered that hummingbirds like to drink a sugar-water mixture for energy. Hoping that Hummer would be thirsty when he awakened, he quickly made up a solution. I found an empty jar lid, and we filled it full and placed it within easy reach of the tiny bird's long beak. He never moved as we worked around him, and his eyes remained tightly shut.

Full darkness now enveloped our yard. Fireflies lighted more than a hundred lanterns, but a time of evening that is usually steeped in quiet beauty for me, I now virtually overlooked. My eyes were focused on Hummer, but no longer through the deepening shadows could I make out any movement of his tiny breast. Somehow I knew in my heart that he still struggled to take his required life breaths.

The silent approach of our black Tortoiseshell cat, KK, coming around the end of the house did somehow catch my eye. KK isn't a hunter by profession, but she is an outdoor cat in the warmer months of the year. Any unusual movement on our patio table in her own backyard, would be sure to tweak her curiosity. If she discovered him, Hummer could become a potential late night snack, or even worse, a cat toy. Neither activity was acceptable, and neither was going to be allowed to happen on my watch that night.

Capturing KK to confine her inside for the rest of the night was my next challenge. To make matters more difficult, KK is one of those cats that never come when you call them. Born a feral cat, she appears when she wants you to do something for her. Catching her would not be easy, but I had no choice but to give it a try.

God, please help me secure KK inside overnight. Calling her name never works, and she is so skittish, she won't come to me if she thinks I want her to do so.

I sat down on the back porch step to ponder methods for

KK's capture. After a very short time, wonder of wonders, KK slowly made her way over to me, walking sedately right underneath the patio table where Hummer rested. As I slowly put out my hand, she actually rubbed up against my knee, and I was able to pick her up and calmly take her inside to her favorite winter retreat in the basement. A small miracle, but I was thankful for it.

One cat down, God, but what about all those other neighborhood cats that cross our property at night? Protect Hummer from them and other predators, please.

About two hours had now passed, and I needed a flashlight to even see Hummer on his wooden stretcher. After shining the light on him for several seconds, I could see a slight movement of his head. He was still alive but I could not stop thinking ahead to tomorrow's prospective burial in the woods.

For some reason I had a strong urge right then to gather for Hummer some of the trumpet flowers that hummingbirds seek to feed from with their long, narrow beaks. Light from the slice of moon and thousands of stars not hidden by street lights in the country, enabled me to make out the flowers in my garden. They were finally perking up their heads in the cooler temperature of the evening. In this light they all looked essentially the same grayish colors, but I remembered where the red and pink ones were located, both favorite colors of all hummingbirds.

I ran around grabbing small lilies and petunias, the only trumpet plants blooming in the garden right now. I hoped that Hummer might regain his strength during the night and suck up their sweet nectar for nourishment. I quietly arranged the flowers around the lid holding the sugar water, placing them as close as I dared to the too quiet little bird.

It was now late, and my husband, who gets up at four a.m. for work, had long ago gone to bed. Before he had gone upstairs he had asked me if I recalled that Bible verse in the Book of Matthew that says, "Who of you by worrying can add a single hour to his life?" Of course I remembered that verse, so why is it so hard for me not to worry? I do know Who is in control of all things, including each and every precious little creature. So now I prayed one last prayer before going up to bed for a few hours of needed rest.

God, please protect Hummer tonight. You knew his name long before us. Such beauty could only have been designed by Your hand. Hummer is Yours. Along with him, I am handing all my worry about him over to You.

Later, following my needed shower, and before finally turning off the light, I again quietly slipped downstairs and went outside to check on Hummer. It was so quiet and so dark, and I didn't want to scare Hummer, so I slowly moved the flashlight beam in his direction. There was something different about him. He had somehow managed to pull his delicate wings in tight against his small body. There was no other indication that he had moved on the board, but this was a very positive sign. I went inside and went to bed. Surprisingly, I fell right to sleep.

When my husband's alarm went off the next morning, I jumped right up and raced down to the kitchen. It was still very dark outside, but using the flashlight, I was able to see through the window that Hummer was still in the same exact position as I had left him before I went to bed, his wings tucked tightly underneath him. I went outside and walked slowly towards the little creature. Suddenly I heard a very soft chirp, then immediately another softer chirp. Hummer was still alive!

O Father, this little creature has made it through the night. Thank You for protecting him. How can I help him now? The sun will come up soon, and it gets hot so fast these days. I don't think he is drinking any of his water, and the flowers I gave him the night before are all wilted. God, please show me what to do.

Right then, the thought about hummingbirds being drawn to the color red was like a neon sign blinking in my head. I ran inside and mixed up another batch of sugar-water in a plastic cup. This time, I put red food coloring in it. I took it outside and I poured it into the lid in front of Hummer's beak until it overflowed. I felt sort of like I was giving communion to a bird.

Meanwhile, as the dawn broke and the sky lightened, and the birds in the trees were greeting the new day, I was trying to decide where to move Hummer to get him out of the already building heat of the rising sun. I had to find a place that was not in dangerous cat territory. Fortunately, our cat KK loves the basement to which she had been banned the previous night, and she was content when I checked on her. She was probably wondering at her good fortune being inside this time of the summer, especially when I delivered fresh food and water to her. Nonetheless, the other neighborhood cats were no doubt still on food patrol, the easier the target, the better.

Having no clear solution in mind for this problem, I went back inside the house to do my morning Bible study. As I was reading the chapter for the day, I felt an urgent need to check on Hummer once again. Since I was upstairs, I went to the back bedroom window, and looked down at the patio table. It was fully light now, and I was immediately able to see there was no bird on the piece of wood on the table. I raced downstairs and outside.

The lid that had held the red sugar-water was completely empty, and so was the board that had been Hummer's stretcher-bed during the night. Hummer was gone. I checked for scattered post cat-meal feathers, but nothing on the table had been disturbed. The wilted flowers were in their same position next to the empty lid. I was ecstatic, and I began shouting words from an old favorite hymn:

"All creatures of our God and King, lift up your voice and with us sing: Alleluia! Alleluia!"

I realized the probability was high that we would never see Hummer again. All the other hummingbirds that visited us the rest of that summer wore the usual drab-colored coats we had gotten used to seeing, and I did not feel the need to give any of them names. We did take down a big red flag in the garage that we thought might have attracted our unique hummingbird friend in for a look around. We also tried to make a habit of keeping the garage doors shut, even when we were home.

There is one thing about which I had no doubts or worries. Wherever Hummer is traveling on his life journey, which thankfully did not end at our home, he is not alone, and perhaps he knows this. Have a wonderful and long life, my tiny friend.

I feel certain he will do just that.

JESSE

A SONG AND A PRAYER

Over the years we have had our share of four-legged "children," mostly cats and dogs. The local animal shelter is where we often traveled when thinking of growing our family. We felt that it was a special privilege to give a home to an unwanted animal. However, my husband had a longing, deep in his heart to replace Buttercup, a little Lhasa Apso friend from his past. Needless to say, that breed of dog is rarely found in an animal shelter, and acquisition is usually accompanied by a hefty fee.

After searching the newspaper fruitlessly for several months, my husband finally saw an advertisement for two, six-month-old Lhasa Apso puppies, and he wasted no time making contact with the seller. A male and a female puppy were waiting for a new home, so he made an appointment for the next Saturday morning to take a "look" at both animals. Our quest for a new fur baby was set to begin, one of us hesitant and the other very enthusiastic.

Is this what You want for us, God? Do You really want us to pay for a dog when there are so many in shelters, free to good homes?

It was a warm, early spring day, when we took our drive to an address fairly close by in a neighboring state. The redbud trees, that for just two short weeks in the spring resplendently decorate the roadside forests in our area, were in their full-blooming purple glory. Most of the other trees along the road were beginning to exhibit various shades of green, as their thousands of buds were no longer willing to wait a moment more for warmer weather. New life was suggested everywhere we looked.

About an hour later, we drove up to a nice-looking townhouse and knocked on the door. It was answered quickly by a young woman who invited us inside. As she opened the door wide for us to enter, I was immediately overwhelmed by an overpowering animal odor coupled with a tinge of disinfectant. Being extremely sensitive to strong odors of any kind, I was tempted to run back to the safety of the car, but I was now as curious about those puppies as my husband. Our greeter took us to the kitchen area where two adorable Lhasa Apso puffs of fur played in a metal crate. The room was clean, and the dogs were clean. Why was I having so much trouble breathing?

The young woman released the puppies from the crate, and they bounded out into the room, excited to be free. They were large for puppies, being already six months old. The female, mostly white with tan, black, and brown splotches, took one look at us, and literally leaped into my husband's open arms. That dog looked as if she had a huge smile on her face, but maybe that was because the classic features of her breed were accompanied by a huge under-bite, a possible reason for her delayed adoption for a considerable fee. There was no such delay this day: an adoption decision was made just like that by my husband, waiting only for a nod from me. Money changed hands, and certification papers were filled out to be mailed to us later. While my husband completed the forms, I was directed to the adjacent room where there were chairs to wait for him.

Immediately on entering the room, I identified the cause of my continued breathing difficulty. In the combined living room and dining room area of the townhouse were various kinds of plastic or wire crates, piled high on each other, and each filled with many cats and kittens of all sizes, colors, ages, and breeds. Having never seen anything like this before in a person's home, I was rather overwhelmed. In fact, I was speechless.

O God, is this why You brought us here, to rescue this puppy already six months old? She needs us right now, and You knew this all along.

My husband quickly finished up the paperwork, and we took our leave of that place, bringing our newest family member with us. We now had my husband's longed-for Lhasa Apso, and my rescue dog all in one. We did not for one minute think it was a coincidence.

Officially, we named her Jessica, but for the next 15 years we called her by her nickname, Jesse. The papers regarding her parentage never did turn up, but that was not important to us since we had no intention of breeding or showing her. As she grew larger than expected over the years, we thought we knew the real reason no official papers ever arrived regarding her heritage. For us, this was not a problem. She was ours, she was family.

Little did we know when we brought Jesse to our home that we had added a vocalist to our household. Soon after her adoption, I began to notice that she would howl in different tones, when she was happy or excited. The dog songs became increasingly frequent and lively as she settled into her new abode.

After returning with her from a long walk one day, I let out a long, high howl to show her I understood her happiness at being outside with companionship. She immediately stopped, cocked her head, and started howling back to me with exactly the same tone and tune. We repeated this sequence many times, and Jesse seemed to have perfect pitch.

A special partnership was formed between us that day. Often, while cooking in the kitchen, I would howl several notes, and Jesse would immediately copy me. This went on for several minutes, sometimes ending in such a rowdy duet that the glasses rattled in the cabinet. What a simple pleasure we shared!

Jesse was not just a singer, she was a "praying" creature. She liked to join prayer time at our weekly Bible Study meeting. After waiting patiently in the adjoining room for us to finish our lesson of the evening, she made her way to the doorway between the rooms. When we all stood and gathered in a prayer circle and clasped hands, Jesse would crawl stealthily on her stomach into the room, right to the edge of our circle. I think she thought she was invisible to the group. This was totally unnecessary on her part for we all enjoyed having her join us. Jessie would put her head down on her front paws, often give a deep sigh, and close her eyes. As we said our prayers out loud, a soft, low, gentle sound, like the quiet murmur of a far away brook, could be heard. Jesse was praying with us. This very soothing sound continued until our final "Amen," when she jumped up to claim welcomed pats on her head. We all came to expect Jesse to join our prayer time each week, knowing the requests of an innocent dog would no doubt be acceptable to the Creator of us all. Jesse prayed with us for many years, and I'm sure God smiled many times in our direction just because of her presence.

Jesse is gone now, but there will always be a special place in my heart for my duet partner, a dog not afraid to sing and to pray.

BOBBY GRAYBIRD

MORNING GREETER

It was early on a morning late in November, the last month of the fall season whose characteristic barren tree branches signal the ultimate, inescapable coming of winter. The sun was still just a thought below the eastern horizon, and the air I breathed in, came out as a cloud of fog around my face. As I walked hurriedly down the driveway to get the morning paper, the security light at the peak of the garage roof lighting my way, a most sociable bird surprised me with a cheery "good morning." He was sitting on a high branch in my favorite hawthorn tree, almost completely concealed by clumps of small orange berries and brown crinkled leaves. I could just make out a round silhouette of gray feathers topped with a black, sleek hood. In a hurry to get to work early as usual, I smiled at the greeting, more to myself than to him, and didn't linger to make a response. Little did I know then that this little bird would become a special part of the beginning of each of my days in the approaching cold and dreary months.

Each morning when the garage door went up, and I went to retrieve the morning paper, that bird would be waiting for me. If I was preoccupied with my own thoughts, usually making plans for the day ahead, he drew my attention to him by hopping hastily from branch to branch and repeatedly calling, his sonorous chirps piercingly clear in the surrounding silence. According to the pictures in the bird book that I had consulted, I thought he most closely resembled a very fat catbird, whose species was known to winter in our mid-Atlantic state. What kind of bird he was didn't really matter in our growing relationship, just as, I am sure, the white color of my hair did not matter to him.

I started calling him Bobby Graybird because he had become more than a casual acquaintance. I would often be already smiling as I slowed down when I passed his perch somewhere in the hawthorn tree, and many times I responded with laughter to his notes of joy and hope for the day ahead of both of us. Eventually, for a few moments every day, I found myself actually talking to him like a known and trusted friend. As the cold, winter days passed, Bobby became more and more visible through the now essentially barren tree branches, with only a few shriveled berries and a rogue leaf here and there remaining to obstruct my view of him.

As our morning time together lengthened into months, so did Bobby's trust in me grow. When I would stop under the hawthorn tree in the morning in response to his summons, he would hop closer and closer onto the lower branches. I knew he probably wanted to tell me the latest bird news, or share some titillating gossip. I didn't have the heart to tell him I really didn't understand "bird talk." Like all good friends, I think he sweetly overlooked my failings, or maybe he was merely unaware of them.

Regardless of the worsening weather, and not considering his own personal needs, Bobby waited for me every morning. Even the ice or snow-covered branches that made a secure foothold impossible for most birds, appeared to be no problem for Bobby. I had long ago checked the tree for any signs of a nest, but there was none; thus, his faithful morning visits had to be planned and carefully scheduled. As far as planning goes, there were times my life's priorities got in the way of our meetings. On those few days that I was unable or late going outside and failed to meet Bobby, I wondered if in his little heart he had missed my visit. I did not relish the thought that he could be sad or lonely because of my absence.

I never did discover where Bobby actually spent the rest of his time after our morning get-togethers. He only came to the hawthorn tree around sunrise, never returning to it as far as I could tell during the rest of the day, though I often checked the branches for his presence. I never saw him gather with other birds at any of the many bird feeders in our backyard, nor did he sing his delightful songs to us from the branches of other trees in our yard.

God, only You know where Bobby goes when he leaves the hawthorn tree. I know You are watching over him, as You watch over all Your creatures, especially the little ones.

Bobby was a very loyal bird friend, and our friendship was rather exclusive. He would never come down to the lower branches when my husband or any other family member tried to coax him to come closer. Even when they tempted him with special treats, like raisins or pumpkin seeds and soft voices, he would remain on a high branch, watching them with his head tilted sideways, a decidedly detached air about him. They all felt completely ignored by my little friend with his beak turned up in the air.

In late March as the winter began to slip away, the hawthorn tree branches responded with subtle changes to the gentle, but deeper strokes of the sun, and the warm spring air that softly began blowing over the earth in our part of the world. The scraggly, long, bare branches began to turn a deep reddish-brown overnight. Tiny buds started to materialize by the thousands, and the few remaining dried-up berries dropped off. Soon the hawthorn tree was covered in a glorious array of tiny, white, lacy flowers, decked out in her annual bridal gown. By now that tree had had at least 20 spring weddings, but this year the special soloist added a superb touch.

As spring progressed, many warm-weather bird friends returned to our yard. None of these birds looked quite like Bobby, and he stayed to himself. Being a loner didn't seem to bother him. He did not even choose to be friends with other catbirds.

God, I know Bobby is Yours and he has purpose. Sometimes I wonder if he could be one of Your earthly messengers. If so, help me to clearly hear and understand what he needs to share.

My few minutes each morning with my little bird friend became a prized part of my day. I came to expect him to be there in our tree, waiting for me to come close to him so we could talk in private. I don't think I took these times for granted, but I am not sure I realized how significant he had become to my life. The brief moments of pleasure with Bobby helped my day get off to a very positive start.

Then one morning Bobby Graybird was not in the hawthorn tree to greet me. Nor did he ever return to say goodbye. He just left. I looked for him for weeks, at all times of the day, but he was gone.

Friends do that sometimes, leave rather suddenly, I mean. Some depart for reasons known, and others for reasons never acknowledged. In either case, the emptiness is usually heartfelt. I really missed my morning visits with Bobby, and I thought about him a lot for a long while, hoping he would just show up again one day. No other bird came to the hawthorn tree to take his place, and slowly I stopped looking for my friend.

What Bobby helped me to understand that winter season of my life is how important it is to cherish all the little gifts we are blessed with each day, because those blessings, including a little puff of gray named Bobby Graybird, may not be around forever.

MONTE MANTIS

THERE IS A WAY HOME

It was the middle of the morning on a bright cerulean summer day. My only planned chore was a quick trip to the grocery store for some essential items not grown in our garden. Never my favorite task, I was anxious to get the grocery shopping over with as early as possible. My grandson was with me, and we were both already extremely hot, the sweat running off of us in tangled rivers. We unloaded our groceries, always twice as many as on our list, from the cart to our car, which had been literally roasting in the heat. Small geysers of steam puffed sporadically into the air from the sun-drenched, newly blacktopped parking area surrounding us. The air itself smelled like new tar, and this was not very pleasant.

My grandson was the first to notice the strange, small, exotic-looking bug on the front windshield of our car. I was able to identify it for him as a baby praying mantis. We watched him as we finished our job, his ongoing yet apparently useless motion becoming the focus of our attention.

Scooting back and forth at an amazing speed across the windshield that had to feel hot, given his shoeless state, this tiny fellow looked like he had places to get to right away. However, each time he got to the side of the windshield, he would stop at the edge and immediately reverse his progress. It seemed he was trying to go somewhere, maybe in response to a summons for adventure, but like many of us, he did not appear to be able to find the right place to take the first step on his journey

We have a rather quirky habit in our family of naming the various wild or domestic non-human friends God brings into our lives. By now, we thought of this little guy as more than a spur-of-the-moment acquaintance, so we bestowed on him the name Monte Mantis. That made it easier to talk to him and about him.

My ongoing conversation with my grandson about this persistent, long-legged bug on our car included the fact that Monte was an insect with wings and could fly away from us any time he chose to do so. I pointed out to my grandson that when I started our car and eventually increased the speed for the drive home, Monte would sooner or later take to the air, leaving the now familiar windshield behind, and end up in a new place to grow up. At first he might be all alone, and that thought was of some concern to us. On the other hand, if he was strong enough to hold on to his launching pad for a while, he could end up in a much safer place to live. Many trees and fields lined the roads to our home, and this change in location, if it occurred, we decided could ultimately be a good thing for Monte. It would provide lots of opportunities for an up-grade in housing, and a chance to find a new family, and make new friends. He probably would even live to a ripe old age in clean, greener, safer surroundings, away from the dangerous bustle of cars coming and going in the busy grocery store parking lot he was currently calling home.

Right then, we decided not to interfere with his fate. In other words, we left him on the windshield of our car, staring through the glass at us, as he continued his trek from one side to the other. We did wonder just what he was thinking or planning.

I started the car and slowly began to work my way out of the parking lot. At this point, Monte stopped his aimless movement, and in fact seemed glued to one spot on the windshield. I stayed in the slower right-hand lane of the roads leading to the highway, hoping that this would help Monte keep out of harm's way of the oncoming traffic if he decided to leave us. As we got further out of town, I had to increase the speed of the car to keep up with the surrounding traffic. My grandson was watching Monte avidly from the back seat. As the car went faster, the increasing force of the wind buffeted the little insect's body. Monte seemed to look directly through the windshield at me, and I guessed if he could talk he could be asking, "What in the world is happening to me? Should I be scared?"

I understood well his growing anxiety. Sometimes in life I had found myself in the midst of a new adventure with no warning or time for preparation. Not knowing where I was going, or where I would end up was a very daunting feeling. Praying for guidance to the One who does know the answer is always a good thing in these situations. I had found myself on my knees more than once over the years.

Dear God, please watch over this little praying mantis and take him safely to a fantastic new home.

The car speed climbed to around 65mph, as I was now driving on the highway. Monte's ability to hold on seemed to weaken. His fragile-looking wings were pummeled viciously by the wind, propelling him closer and closer to the edge of the windshield. Both my grandson and I were getting extremely uneasy about the seemingly imminent conclusion of Monte's ride with us. With now squinting eyes, Monte still seemed to watch us through the windshield, just as closely as we watched him. It was like he was trying to communicate to us, maybe begging us to take care of him. I still stayed in the slower lane of traffic, next to the waving fields and beckoning trees, but the car was moving rather fast for its little passenger.

Oh God, this little praying mantis has come so far; please help him to safely reach a better place on this earth, and let this adventure end well for him. Let our unscripted part in it be a blessing.

The exit from the highway toward our home finally came into view after about five very long miles, which due to my heightened tension and concern for Monte, seemed to last more like 30 miles. Monte was still managing somehow to hold on at the edge of the windshield. I am sure he was using all his might. As I slowed the car and made the turn off of the highway, Monte seemed to immediately relax his tiny body, as if giving a sigh of relief. I came to a full stop at the blinking red light at the first intersection. Suddenly, Monte disappeared from our view. Nature's bounty was beckoning on all sides of us now, and many favorable locations were available for a new home for our tiny friend. Monte had apparently decided on this place for his future address. We wished him a rousting and happy "goodbye and good luck." My grandson and I were both smiling and we felt really good, like we had actually been used in a special way to help one of God's little creatures find a better place to live.

I was in fact humming as I turned up the final hill to our home. Suddenly, a tiny movement at the top of the windshield caught my eye. Slowly but surely, a small, determined praying mantis began his descent of the windshield once again. Incredibly, Monte was still with us. We pulled the car into our driveway and hopped out. Monte slowly pushed himself up straight and tall, for a baby praying mantis that is, and looked around as if to say, "Now this is where I wanted to go all along on my adventure. This is where I am meant to spend the rest of my life." Monte then climbed up on the top of the car, saluted us with his long front leg, and then stood very still, looking slowly from side to side. Perhaps he was gathering strength for the beginning of the rest of his life. His new world included trees of all shapes and sizes, green grass, and flowers of all varieties and colors, perhaps a paradise for a little praying mantis who had been growing up in a parking lot.

Several minutes later, after we had unloaded the groceries and had taken them into the house to be put away or refrigerated, we went back outside to check on Monte. He was gone from the windshield as well as from the top of the car. We carefully searched for him, but this time he really was not to be found.

A very independent baby praying mantis had hitched a ride to our home. We knew he was where he was supposed to be, exploring his new habitat, looking for friends and maybe a family to adopt him, and continuing an adventure that had started only a few minutes before on that same morning.

"Welcome to your new home, Monte; stay as long as you like," my grandson and I shouted as we turned to go back inside the house. "We hope you have a great life, and maybe we will meet again this summer!"

With God, all things are possible.

TAFFY

MIKE, GAY AND JENNY

HEATED DECISION

Our short-haired tabby cat, named Taffy for her luscious caramel color, was taking her approaching motherhood rather serenely. We knew her waiting period would soon be over, since her swollen abdominal area, so full of tiny baby kittens, was practically skimming the floor as she waddled slowly from room to room in our home. Like pregnant females in many species during their last couple of days prior to delivery, she looked very misshapen and to us very uncomfortable. In fact, Taffy's body, between her head and her tail, was so large, all three of us children were certain we were each going to have at least one baby kitten to name and claim for our own for a few weeks until other families adopted them.

It was the middle of a glorious summer, and the days were long, hot, and very humid. There was little relief from the heat, even when the sun bid its "goodnight" in the western sky. Our family had not yet installed air conditioning, which many of us take for granted today. We sought other ways to stay cool, especially at night, such as sleeping with just a sheet and pillow on the smooth, cool, hardwood floors. Our basement was also very tempting for respite from the heat, but it was far away from the security of our parents, and they had no trouble sleeping in their room upstairs on the second floor.

Occasionally, my brother and sister and I would move our bedding outside to the narrow balcony that ran across the back of our house. There we would hope to be cooled by a gentle stroke from a passing breeze. As we gazed up at the familiar constellations in the blackened dome above us, on some nights those stars seemed close enough for us to reach out and touch. The Milky Way was often a visible stripe in the sky, especially when the moon was in its early crescent stage. Each of us vied to be the first one to spot one of the many shooting stars which seemed so abundant in the summer, and were a symbol to all of us of good luck, and a time for making wishes. Maybe we saw more of the shooting stars back then just because we took the time to look for them. I know our wishes were usually very simple, and lately had focused on Taffy delivering at least three baby kittens.

Taffy, who was a people-lover like most tabby cats, was usually with one of us, so it had not been difficult to keep a close watch on her as her time to deliver drew nearer. Our whole family anxiously anticipated her coming birthing event.

However, one morning when we awoke, none of us could find our little mother-to-be anywhere. Our mother suspected Taffy had found a hiding place in the house to have her kittens. We set out to search in all directions, because, if at all possible, we wanted to quietly witness those kittens being born. We looked in all the corners, and all the closets, and in any place that we would disappear in our frequent games of hide and seek. We could not find our cat. Mother then decided Taffy must have slipped outside when our father left for work, seeking a quiet, safe place to deliver her babies. A thorough search beneath the bushes, in the gardens filled with flowers, inside the window wells, and in the unattached garage, yielded no pregnant cat. Calls to Taffy brought no response.

The minutes that morning passed slowly, and our concern for Taffy's well-being became more intense. We found ourselves looking for her in the same spots over and over. As the sun steadily climbed higher, the day got hotter and hotter. We just couldn't imagine where Taffy could be. Her food and water bowls went untouched.

Feeling defeated, we sat in the kitchen with cool drinks, rehashing our missing cat problem. Our mother asked if any of us had checked in the attic. Of course not, none of us had looked there because we were forbidden to venture up there in the summer without permission. With no insulation under the dark shingled roof, the air in the attic became so oppressive it seemed to scorch your lungs as you took in a breath. Going up into the attic during a summer day felt like what it must be to enter a fiery furnace. We knew it was not safe. Mother did, however, use the bottom landing on the attic steps to store extra paper goods, towels, and other miscellaneous items for easy access. The attic door had one of those latches that would close, but seemed to open magically at times by itself. We had all been instructed to push the door shut, if ever we saw it was open. This we did unconsciously as we walked by the door.

We looked at each other, all having the same thought at the same moment. Was it even possible that Taffy had somehow gotten into the attic in her quest for a private place to deliver her kittens? None of us remembered shutting that door recently. Mother decided to check anyway, primarily because we had looked everyplace else. We all followed her quickly up the stairs.

The door to the attic looked tightly closed. When Mother opened it, there on the landing, in the middle of a pile of towels, were Taffy and four newly born kittens, all hardly breathing due to the intensity of the heat. Mother, who taught science at the local junior high school and was known as a problem solver, grabbed the towel the kittens were lying on and ran down to the kitchen, while directing me, the oldest, to grab Taffy. I gently lifted our limp cat, and we all followed closely on Mother's heels down the stairs.

In the kitchen we found some old medicine droppers in a drawer (does anyone have a bunch of these lying around anymore?) and all of us started slowly feeding Taffy and her kittens tiny drops of tepid water. We all understood this was not a time to hesitate or question our response.

Looking back, I realize this was one of those times God's Hand worked a miracle in my life. We did not know what we were doing, but He did. Slowly but surely, the baby kittens started to breathe more easily as they cooled down. Their eyes were tightly shut, and they started making tiny little mewing sounds, so welcome to all of us. The kittens must have been just a few minutes old when we found them. Taffy recovered quickly with fluids, and became anxious about all the help she was receiving with her new family.

After we were certain our expanded cat family all had a chance to survive, we made a bed of the towels from the attic in a corner of the cool basement, the spot that would have been the optimal delivery suite. We watched from the basement steps as Taffy lay down, and somehow, guided by natural instinct, all the kittens scooted around until they had latched on and started to drink their mother's milk. It was very satisfying to see them all moving and drinking. What a beautiful sight they all made together. Since there were four, we each got to name one, as we had wished, and jointly named the fourth together.

Eventually, we were able to find good homes for three

of the kittens, and we kept one little black calico boy kitten named Puddin, so Taffy would not be lonely. Mother also made sure that Taffy and Puddin would have no more kittens.

We talked about this event for years, always with wonder that God had to have been the One to direct our mother to the attic steps, just in time to save the lives of all of the kittens, as well as Taffy. My father put a secure lock high on the attic door to ensure nothing like that would ever happen again. Taffy and Puddin shared our lives for many years, treasured members of our family.

TAPPER

SCARLET WONDERS

Winter's white decor in the country, often a combination of multiple deliveries of snow and ice, is the perfect backdrop for birds of scarlet, commonly known as cardinals. These brilliant birds, at least the males of the species, proudly wear their ruby-red robes with matching pointed crowns, and constantly fill the air with their pure, titillating songs. Several friends have cardinal pictures on their January calendars, associating these birds with hopefulness and good luck in the new year. Others have small, red-tinted glass or pottery replicas tucked into the corners of their homes, providing splashes of crimson where a cheerful, decorative contrast is desirable.

A few of these dazzling, crimson vocalists dare to settle in our area year-round, while the habit of most of our feathered resident bird friends is to leave the neighborhood in the late fall to seek more hospitable climates for the impending colder months. The brave cardinals that elect to stay seem willing to accept, the cold weather's changing menu of inescapable below-freezing temperatures, and the bouts of blowing snow and chilling winds that sometimes pester us well into March. In fact, cardinals seem to revel in these frosty offerings, often flitting from silver branch to silver branch, always singing boisterously their approval of their good fortune.

At times, flocks of these royally garbed birds pass through our vicinity on their way to other destinations. In the bleak winter landscape they are easy for both child and adult to recognize. It is a moment of profound beauty to see a small tree whose leafless branches are covered with new, pure-white snow, bedecked with a multitude of hopping balls of crimson, all harmonizing at the top of their voices, their notes as clear as the sounding of the chimes from the nearby church steeple. The sight is a wonder never to be forgotten, a musical postcard of winter delight that seals itself forever in the mind of those fortunate enough to witness it.

Oh God, thank You for moments of beauty so intense that we never forget them, and are able to replay and enjoy them over and over in our minds wherever life takes us.

When snow covers the ground and nature's banquet is buried from sight of all creatures, we make sure all of our birdfeeders are full of seeds, berries, and nuts. Visiting birds of all sizes and shapes stop for ready refreshment and a break from their journeys, but only the cardinals return faithfully day after day for their anticipated morning and evening meals. At times, a pushy blue-jay may attempt to take over the cardinal's number one spot in the pecking order at the feeders; otherwise, most of the little chubby black and white juncos that somehow mysteriously show up when it snows, and the few stragglers we think are brown-striped sparrows and faded red or yellow finches, are happy to share an occasional nourishing meal in peace.

The easily identified bright male cardinals are almost always accompanied by their faithful mates, often described by observers as either drab or dowdy. Although her presence is suspected, even when searched for, the female cardinal is usually very difficult to detect. Her feathers of dark, faded shades of browns, with just a hint of deep-red tinge on the tip of her pointed crown and the edges of her wings and tail, allow her to almost magically disappear into the bare branches of winter. In the other seasons, when the green or colored leaves fill in the empty spaces on the branches of bushes and trees, she is completely hidden from the casual sight of humans, as well as from detection by natural predators. Nature has a perfectly good reason for the clothing discrepancy for these bird mates, wanting to ensure the safety of the wife and mother during the mating season and while she nurtures her young. However, I do wonder if she ever yearns to wear clothes brighter than a Christmas poinsettia like her mate, just once in her life.

Year after year, a favorite nesting place for our wintering cardinals is deep inside one of the giant holly trees that stand guard at each end of our home. Planted over 30 years ago when we first moved here, they are stuffed full of shiny, dark, forest-green leaves that stay on the tree all year round. Dotted with thousands of white blossoms in the spring, and hundreds of red berries in the fall and winter, these trees make perfect castles for royal cardinal couples.

One fall, a very unique cardinal and his mate chose our yard in which to settle and make a home for the coming winter. They chose the most spacious holly tree by the stone chimney to build their snug nest that would shelter them from even the harshest blizzard. So dense were the protective leaves surrounding their home, only an observer specifically watching their activity for long periods of time, would recognize it as their residence.

On one particularly frigid morning as I was fixing my breakfast, I heard a curious tap, tap, tapping on the decorative glass kitchen window overlooking the drooping rhododendrons and azalea bushes at the back of the house. Quickly turning, I saw a bright red bird, with jet black eyes that seem to sparkle, who nodded to me, tapped again on the window, then quickly flew away. I had actually heard of this tapping gesture by cardinals happening to others, but this is the first time I had my own personal scarlet greeter.

From that day on, my early morning routine seemed to become my new bird friend's morning routine. Whenever I fixed my breakfast, he would fly to the shallow window sill, and tap his cheerful greeting to me against the glass. After a week of these continuous brief but pleasant interchanges, I named him "Tapper," and like my other friends, I looked forward to his visits. In fact, I had a hard time patiently waiting for the sun to rise in the morning at its later winter time, since its golden rays seemed to give my little red friend permission to begin his day with me.

O God, I am so thankful for the little bird You sent my way. He asks nothing in return for his gifts of lively songs, and splashes of color that add moments of marvel in a world in the doldrums of winter. His tapping speaks to me of Your presence in the changing tapestry outside my window.

Tapper only came to "our" window early in the day, and stayed just long enough to get my attention and tap his "good morning" code. I would quickly greet him and explain how much I appreciated his first light tapping. I thanked him each day by placing a few raisins on the patio table, right outside the kitchen door. After tapping his hello and nodding his pointed head to me several times, he would tap his goodbye, and swoop over to eat his raisins. Often he glanced back over his wing to make sure he was not going to be disturbed, or be asked to share his treat. He would then leave for various bird duties, his morning salutation to me finished for the day. We followed this routine daily until late spring of that year, when without a goodbye tap or nod, he and his mate left our yard. Maybe they were searching for a bigger castle. I will never know for sure.

As far as I know, I have not encountered Tapper since he left, though over the years several of his relatives have come to visit or to board in his holly tree. It is possible that Tapper and his mate returned to the area but had other more important chores to perform in the morning than to greet an old friend. However, I choose to think he is somewhere else, brightening another person's life, once he gets their attention.

Tapper was an unexpected gift that winter. His presence reminded me to be on the alert for the little things in life that are sent my way by the Creator Himself, to make me smile and bring me moments of simple pleasure. A bright scarlet relative of Tapper's might come your way one day to sing, tap, or nod his good morning to you. Don't miss his greeting, or think his visits are by chance. Pay attention to what he has to teach you, and remember to say "thank you" to the Sender.

BANDIT AND DIXIE

DOGs - DOGS ON GUARD

Bandit and Dixie are the fur-babies of the couple who live in the house positioned directly across the street from our mailbox located at the end of our driveway. These dogs are medium-sized Australian shepherds who hide their true identities by looking very similar to the more familiar breed of collies. This ability to naturally become incognito is very important because they are not just ordinary pets. From the time their owners leave for work, well before the darkness of night has lifted, until their return late in the afternoon, Bandit and Dixie are extremely busy. These dogs watch over all the activities taking place directly in front of their big bay window. In fact, what may seem like a dull, boring job to others, requires a high degree of conscientiousness and fortitude, ultimately helping ensure the well-being of the entire neighborhood. Even their owners have no idea of their pets' level of responsibilities. The true importance of their job is understood by a very small, elite unit, of which Bandit and Dixie are members. They are acknowledged by a select few as belonging to DOGs, a covert group known to only those who have a need to know as DOGS ON GUARD.

Day after day these brave animals scrutinize the unannounced arrivals of FedEx delivery persons, yard maintenance workers, utility meter readers, or mail delivery persons. They also watch for neighbors, some with shifty-looking pets, and others with innocent-looking children whose shouts of glee and wonder never fool the DOGs.

Then there are those sneaky cats that think they own the neighborhood. They glide past on a schedule so random that Bandit and Dixie have to be ready at a moment's notice to fulfill their sworn duty. All intruders are considered potentially dangerous until proven otherwise, and each occurrence is a new call to action.

And just what is it that DOGs members do when their protocol is activated by one of these intruders? This is a question whose answer many would want clarified if they even suspected a tiny bit of what really goes on daily behind that innocuous-looking bay window across the street. DOGs is an agency of exceptional canine spies, similar to man's Central Intelligence Agency (CIA) in the United States, except that DOGs' active members all have four feet. There is no end to the hours of watching, waiting, and sedentary patrolling that Bandit and Dixie must perform to do their job correctly, and implementation of the DOGs protocol is never to be taken lightly.

The appearance of any of the aforementioned potentially threatening intruders requires immediate and fierce barking along with strenuous howling! This is almost always accompanied by the furious banging of paws and heads against the window panes when the DOGs protocol is fully activated. Any reaction to this behavior by one of their targets results in an instantaneous upgrade to the response effort to show intruders that their responses have indeed not gone unnoticed. More barking and banging ensue until the threat resolves, and the intruder leaves the area, often with a shaking of their head, and a rather puzzled look on their face.

This process I have personally witnessed from my home time after time. As one of the daily "intruders" to the area overseen by Bandit and Dixie, it might be thought after several years that my identification category had been changed from "intruder" to "frequent caller," if not "friend." Some might expect that after such an extended length of time, things would remain passive and quiet when the dogs see it is me approaching my mailbox day after day. There are top secret reasons why this is not the way the program works. Let me explain what I am allowed.

Our local newspaper is delivered early in the morning before sunrise seven days a week. This is perfect timing for me because my husband and I get up each day around four a.m. After he leaves for work, I begin my favorite time of day, which includes prayer time and sipping my hot chocolate while watching the dawn break into the colors of the day along the eastern horizon.

When I am absolutely sure that the paper has been delivered, there comes what I shall refer to as "prep time" with Dixie and Bandit. At around 6:45 a.m., shortly after the dog's owners have left for work, and the school bus has pulled out with its first student load of the day, I push the button to open the garage door. I step outside and look up and down the street very carefully, searching for any movement or unsuspected activity. I am usually in my pajamas, but even with a cover-up, I don't want to be surprised by other early morning risers out taking a walk. If things are quiet on the street, I begin my slow, stealthy descent to the edge of the driveway. There our mailbox with the attached paper holder is located right in the center of the area Bandit and Dixie have designated for DOGs' *modus operandi*.

All the while I am walking, I am wondering if the DOGs daily shift has begun. Are Dixie and Bandit invisible just below the ledge of their bay window, listening for the first intruder of the day? I check to see if the long white curtains in the window are even slightly moving. No movement is visible yet today, very good. When I reach my destination, I deliberately turn my back to the bay window, and slowly and silently pull the paper out of its mailbox holder. Then I check the mailbox for mail not taken in the day before, or a possible note left by a neighbor. Then suddenly I slam the mailbox door shut tight with a loud bang.

That's all it takes! A frenzy of excited barking pelts against my back. I quickly turn around, facing where Bandit and Dixie appear to be trying to bang the panes out of the bay window. I calmly step into the middle of the still deserted street, throw my hands up high, and give them the double victory sign. The cacophony of barking that accompanies this motion is intense, even louder than I had previously heard. I slap my hands on my thighs quickly several times, and jump up and down in the middle of the road. I know if anyone is watching me from behind a curtained window, they might suppose I am probably losing it. That foolish kind of thinking is often directed at those of us with white hair.

The barking peaks and then just as quickly stops as I turn and begin my walk back up the driveway to my house, the paper in hand. "Good job," I whisper, and send a confidential signal with my hands behind my back, to the dogs still watching me steadily from their bay window. "You are definitely ready for today's challenges!"

To clarify further, the real reason I am at the mailbox this early each morning is to make sure that the DOGs are ready for their day's assignment to begin. Only Bandit and Dixie and I know that what just happened is their rehearsal before the true intruders advance into DOGs territory. Even if we were forced to tell anyone about our clandestine jobs, no one would believe the important responsibilities of dogs that look like friendly collies, and a mature, sedate, white-haired woman.

I have a feeling anyone reading this story is rolling their eyes right now in disbelief. Actually, Bandit, Dixie, and I most appreciate the many inherent skeptics and doubters who pass by the big bay window. It makes it easier to keep our jobs top secret.

"Goodbye, my furry friends. Your mission is still safe, and so is the neighborhood. Keep up the good work!" My smile is wide as I close the garage door. I think it will be another really fine day. The DOGs on our street are ready for duty.

Thank you, God, for the fun Your creatures provide us if we let our imagination soar.

LONESOME DOVE AND THE HAWK

IN THE BLINK OF AN EYE

It was still fairly early in the morning on one of those hot, steamy August days. A few wispy cloud shapes dotted the deep, cobalt-domed ceiling over the distant hills to the west of our home in the country. To the east, the brilliant sunrise that had announced the arrival of morning, at least to us, had faded from gold, blues and pinks to the intense bluish color we had come to expect from a shimmering summer sky. There was no doubt the sun would be in control of today's weather. Already the heated air was extremely humid, and breathing it seemed to take some conscious effort. An occasional tease from a slight breeze made it just barely worthwhile to remain outside during the break my husband and I had taken from gardening.

As we relaxed in the shade on our patio and sipped cool, refreshing water, our favorite dove friend arrived to eat her first meal of the day. She landed so close to where we were sitting that we were very careful to talk quietly and move little, so as not to frighten her away. She is well known to us, having been a faithful visitor to our yard in the spring, summer, and fall months during the last six years. She has been on her own since she lost her mate to an accident of fate in our yard three years ago. Doves mate for life, so though she returned to our yard around March each year with other dove couples, she always stays by herself when eating, or when leaving to fly away to wherever doves go to spend their life minutes. Knowing her history, and presuming her sadness, we had long ago named her "Lonesome Dove."

Time seemed to pass slowly as we rested, though I realize this is human perception, not something that really happens. We lazily watched as the leaves feebly waved to us, barely stirring high up in the trees. The neighbors all seemed to be sleeping late in the early heat; no one else was outside, as far as we could see. The quiet was blissful, a short respite before weed whackers and lawn mowers would take over the neighborhood weekend.

I slowly turned in my chair to check if Lonesome Dove was still eating. At that exact moment with no warning of any kind, a brown rolling mass of feathers hurtled itself seemingly right at us from high in the sky. It resembled what I thought a brown lightning bolt would look like if I were its target. Slicked-back, dark feathers in the shape of a missile slammed into the earth in front of me with such force that I was sure I felt the ground itself shake. In the time it took me to blink my incredibility, that source of mighty power soared back into the sky at the same top speed, its long talons curled in tight toward its body. It passed so close to my husband still turned away from the action, that he felt as if his shoulder had been touched by some invisible spirit. As we both jumped to our feet, he shouted, “What just happened?”

In that split second of time, all that was left of where Lonesome Dove had been calmly eating her breakfast, were a few gray feathers floating slowly in the air. My mouth hung open and I pointed to those feathers now beginning to settle peacefully on the ground. My mind could not seem to catch up with what my eyes had just witnessed. As I was explaining to my husband what had occurred, our eyes desperately searched the yard and the sky for any sign of Lonesome Dove. The only moving thing we could see was a huge brown hawk gliding back and forth in his unconcerned, lazy flight pattern.

Our precious little dove friend was gone. I felt numb. I have learned through past experiences that life's path can be altered over time for good or for bad by a subtle twist of fate here, or an unconscious turn there. However, the occurrences have been rare where I have actually witnessed the phenomena take place in seconds right before my eyes.

We relived the event, telling it over and over to each other, while continuing our fruitless search of the yard for Lonesome Dove. Constantly shaking our heads in disbelief did not help us accept any better what had happened on that normally calm, peaceful grassy spot beside our patio. In a way, though, talking about our feelings to each other did help us through a stage I can only describe as mourning for the loss of our little friend.

The next day dawned as usual, bright and clear, and already hot. Many colorful birds were at our feeders, but no solitary gray dove was on the grass, gleaning the seeds dropped by the others.

O God, You alone know all about each of Your creatures, even the needs of small gray doves. Thank You that we don't need to carry that burden of responsibility ourselves.

As it always does, life goes on after seeming to have paused, or even stopped for moments hard to define, mostly for reasons not known and not understood. That day was filled to the brim with chores and passed rather quickly. It ended with a light supper for us at the kitchen table as we finally began to relax.

My husband began to gather the dishes to rinse them in the sink, when suddenly in a loud whisper he called me to come quickly to the kitchen window. He was pointing outside to the grassy area under the feeders. There, calmly eating her supper as usual, was a solitary gray bird we both knew immediately, without a doubt, had to be our Lonesome Dove. There was no way to get close to her without scaring her, but from what I could see from our kitchen window, her feathers were a little ruffled in spots, but generally intact. She seemed steady on her feet as she shuffled to and fro, focused on eating her dinner, her head bobbing naturally up and down as she selected her preferred seeds. She did not appear at all afraid, never once even looking back over her wing as if fearful of a potential brown menace.

We looked at each other. Where had she been for the last day and a half? How did she escape her captor with the long sharp talons? How could it possibly even be her? And yet, somehow we knew in our hearts that the little gray bird was indeed our Lonesome Dove. The facts backed us up: all the other dove visitors we had had this year had arrived in pairs; there were no other single doves under the feeders; only Lonesome Dove came day after day to eat her meals alone, never with a particular friend or mate. We wanted so much to believe that it was her that we did not have to work particularly hard to convince each other that simply a miracle had occurred.

To this day we still have many unanswered questions about what happened between the swift-flying brown predator and the innocent gray bird. As in so many things in life here on earth, there will never be definitive answers to our questions. We only have our random speculation about what took place from the time Lonesome Dove disappeared from our yard, until the time she returned, acting as if nothing out of the ordinary had happened. But that did not change our gratitude for the ending of this story. Lonesome Dove is alive and well, and back home in our yard. She still visits us on her own each year, with no apparent worries about her future.

Thank You, God, for protecting our little gray friend. When she leaves us in the fall to go wherever she spends the months away from us, please keep her safe. And if it is in Your plan, bring her back to us again next spring.

FARAWAY MOON

MOON-NIGHT VISITORS

I live just a few miles from the town where I was born and in which I grew up. Our home is on a little over an acre of what used to be farmland, complete with a small woods and a smaller, clear area just the perfect size for a garden. It is within easy reach of a highway that can take me quickly back to the town. I knew this property was special the first time I walked under its majestic oaks and tulip poplars in their full summer glory. They were scattered among the numerous varieties of nut trees that stood guard in the winding farm path that would eventually become my backyard. It was a place I could right away call home, and after more than 30 years, I still feel the same sense of peace that I felt that very first day.

Ten minutes into the countryside made all the difference in the variety of animals that pass through our yard, as compared to our older home in the town with its numerous cement and blacktop boundaries. In fact, prospective visits from four-legged small and large visitors were some of the reasons that cemented the decision of our family to move to this inviting location.

Though some of the wild animal visits happen in the daylight, most make their appearance at the quiet times of dawn and dusk, or during a night lit only by the moon and the stars, since there is not a single streetlight in sight. For the most part, these creature visits are quick and delightful, though some of the squirrels and rabbits feel they have squatter's rights. There is nothing like seeing the unexpected full-antlered buck and his doe soar over a fence of weathered wood or stone left from the old farm's days, or hear a flock of wild turkeys gobble their way through the yard. These friends usually do not pause long enough to even say hello, and ask for nothing but to share a path through our little piece of the earth. We feel blessed when we do get to see them, especially on moonlit nights, when it seems like the Creator Himself must send out the invitations on our behalf. As for our visitors, they probably just assume that they will always be welcome, since we are living on property that has been used by their families for untold periods of time.

One summer, however, several years ago, some of our nocturnal animal guests caused some mischief and gave us a few anxious moments, and though short- lived, a few misgivings about country living.

The first moon-night visitor that summer was a possum. Because I had the air conditioner running during the night with the window almost closed, I did not realize that we had had company until daylight broke the next morning. Gazing down into our generally serene backyard from an upstairs window, which is part of my usual morning routine, I stared in disbelief. I thought what I was seeing looked as if some sort of devil-wind had swirled through our yard, disguising it as an aggravated artist's rendition of an untended garbage dump.

Trash cans were knocked over, and a week's worth of plastic bags of various colors and sizes were in shredded disarray around the yard, some bags even hanging on branches of some of the trees. Their contents were strewn out from them in all directions, each bag looking like it had exploded and died on the spot. What a horrific mess! It took me hours to pick up all the tissues, aluminum cans, bottles, all kinds of odds and ends we had tossed away, as well as the numerous old food items, many showing signs of being recently sampled. At the time, I did not know the responsible party behind this trash disaster, but it didn't take us long to identify the culprit.

After the sun dipped below the horizon that evening, my husband and I started flicking on the outside lights every time we walked into the kitchen, each time doing a quick visual inspection of the yard. Persisting in this routine for two more nights paid off. Swaying from a long, low branch that had been begging all summer for something to use it as a swing, was the guilty party. A large, sleek, gray possum was hanging by his tail, and, he was not alone. On another lower branch of the same tree, hung a slightly smaller version, and clinging to her were two baby possums. Our uninvited visitor from two nights previously had brought company back with him this time to his new outdoor restaurant, hoping for another wonderful gastronomical experience, this time for the whole family.

They were going to be disappointed. We had tightly closed our security locks on the lids of the garbage cans so there were no food items available for them to feast on, or other items to enjoy dispersing throughout the yard. Not feeling a bit guilty about bringing to a halt their desire to stuff themselves and play at our expense, we wished them goodnight, and hopefully goodbye. We caught glimpses of them scurrying through the yard once or twice over the next week or two around dusk, and occasionally found the trashcans knocked over in the morning, but the lid locks held secure, and there were no more nouveau art garbage displays in the yard that summer.

O God, all Your creatures are important to You. Help us to treasure their visits, even if they are not always perfect guests.

Later that same summer, two tidy raccoon visitors began making a habit of passing through our yard. Our sightings of them were generally in the early evening, or at the breaking of the dawn, so I guess we missed the moonlight dances they held. The raccoons were tree lovers, and one or more of our many nut trees seemed to be routinely dropping their favorite bounty just for them. For some reason we had nuts in abundance that year, as acorns, beechnuts, hickory nuts, and walnuts allowed the raccoons to enjoy feasting as their palates desired. The raccoons were cute with their black masks, striped tails, and tiny feet. They were fun to watch when they stopped to eat, although we never saw them during the day when we were outside doing various chores.

As the summer advanced, the raccoons appeared more often, sometimes even arriving in the daylight. They began to act as though the yard belonged to them, and started chasing our dog and cat in surprise attacks. This became worrisome, not just for our pets, but because we had grandchildren who visited often, and loved playing in the yard on the huge tire swing. In fact, with all the activity in our yard, we could not figure out why the raccoons did not seek the nearby quiet wooded area, with a little winding stream available for their well known food washing requirements. It took seeing them disappear one evening into a round, dark hole high in a hollow walnut tree branch to finally convince us the raccoons were no longer just visiting. They had staked a claim on our yard for their summer residence, and we suspected they might have brought the rest of their family with them.

We had heard the often repeated warnings about raccoons possibly carrying rabies in our county, and with the status change from raccoon visitors to raccoon residents, and perhaps aggressors, our concern for the safety of our grandchildren and pets became our first priority. We had no choice but to call an Animal Removal Specialist (ARS) to take charge of our uninvited boarders.

The ARS arrived the next day with a long extension ladder. Sure enough, thirty feet up in the huge black walnut tree in their snug little home, were four baby raccoons sound asleep. Wearing protective gloves and face protection, the ARS retrieved the baby raccoons, gently placing them in a canvas pouch, and descended the ladder. No adult raccoons were in sight during this activity, so he then set up a cage under the tree, hoping to trap the missing parents. He left, taking the raccoon babies with him. We had contacted this particular animal rescuer because he released the animals in his care into approved wilderness areas throughout the county. He assured us the baby raccoons were big enough to make it on their own, even if the parents could not be found to join them.

For one week we watched the cage, but nothing entered it. We were told to change the food used as bait, but that made no difference in the outcome—nothing. We became more concerned about the possibility of our own dog and cat, whom we had restrained in the house during most of this time, entering the cage to get at the food. We called the ARS to come and collect his trap. No sightings were made of any more raccoons the rest of that summer. The tension in the backyard evaporated, and we felt safe sending our grandchildren and pets out there to play. We often discussed how the raccoon parents could possibly have known their family was no longer in our tree, but of course they probably checked things out many times when we were not watching.

I would have liked to have been able to reassure them that their babies were safe.

O God, we know You are in charge of all Your creatures, both big and small. We meant no harm to the raccoon family, but at the same time, we needed to protect our family. Sometimes life's choices are not easy to make. Guide us in making the best decisions for all involved, now and in the future.

The third moon-night caller that summer was a relative of the famous French animal cartoon character called Pepé LePew, a skunk of international fame. Several people in our neighborhood caught glimpses of a black-and-white chubby animal skirting across their porch or patio in the moments between dusk and the approaching darkness. It is a time of day when shapes are still visible outside, and the colors of the day, though muted, are not yet swallowed up by the black of night. We had been watching for the animal presumed to be a skunk, but never saw one in our yard.

I like fresh air, even when the sultry, sweltering nights of summer make sleeping difficult without the air conditioner running. I usually crack open one or two of the windows in my room to let in just a little of that sweet country air. One night I awoke from a deep sleep, choking and gagging. Momentarily, I thought I might be having a heart attack, but then I immediately identified the awful smell that had overwhelmed me as skunk "perfume." I felt as if I were being strangled by an indiscernible prowler.

There is nothing else like the distinctive smell of a skunk. It is so specific, no one ever mistakes it for the smell of a porcupine, or a groundhog, or anything else. No, a skunk smell, once learned, is unchanging and usually considered extremely offensive. Coughing mightily by now,

I jumped out of bed and closed the windows, but by now the pungent smell had permeated the whole house. I couldn't air out the house because the disgusting odor was coming in from the outside. It took several hours to eliminate the offensive odor by turning the air-conditioning fan on full-blast. My coughing eventually abated, as my husband slept soundly through the entire event.

From that night, through the rest of the summer, keeping the windows open was no longer an option for me, regardless of my yearning for fresh air. Closed windows prevented the skunk smell from getting inside the house, but when I went out for the newspaper in the morning, more often than not I was greeted by that familiar noxious odor. That skunk really knew how to effectively use his atomizer. Other than de-freshening the air, the skunk caused us no problems.

Despite the recurring smell over the final weeks of summer, we had no more sightings of our perfume deliverer. Neither had our neighbors reported further sightings of the skunk, though they also occasionally experienced his familiar lingering odor.

Then one evening around firefly time, just as I opened the patio door to refill the cat's water dish, there on our back porch step stood a beautiful coal-black animal, with a brilliant white stripe down the center of his head and back. Needless to say, he got my immediate attention, just as I quickly got his. He was not very big, and I thought he had to be a relative of the skunk seen earlier in the season by my neighbors. Hearing and seeing me open the door, he quickly disappeared into the thick azaleas and rhododendron plants next to the porch. The noble thing was that he took his perfume atomizer with him without using it.

I saw him a little later sauntering through the backyard, and I wondered if he was lost. I hoped he knew where he was going and that it was far away from here. I had heard that skunks spray other animals that become too curious about them. I was concerned that our dog or cat might try to make his acquaintance if they spied him in their own backyard. It was funny, but after that night, we did not see that skunk again, though occasionally he or one of his relatives left a perfumed calling card. Maybe he found a friendlier welcome in someone else's yard.

O God, I know this animal with his identifiable black and white fur coat and unique smell belongs to You. Please guide him into a safe place to spend the summer days, and let it be far away from our home.

The visits of the possums, the raccoons, and the skunk callers that summer kept things rather lively at our country home. The night creatures that visited each had a role, if small, to play in my life story. Remembering their antics now makes me smile. I'm not sorry they came my way.

CLINGER

HOLD ON TIGHT

It was the earliest spring I could ever remember. The preceding winter had been soft and gentle, like a woman on her knees quietly meditating. Snow and ice storms, so common in our area, were almost non-existent. The few snow-filled clouds that did pass over occasionally dropped a few flakes, briefly covering the ground with a thin white blanket, then quickly disappeared, somehow knowing their existence was to be short-lived this year. Much to the children's dismay, there was not one "snow day," an unscheduled reprieve when the schools close because of bad weather. Sledding, snowball fights, red cheeks, and big cups of hot chocolate and marshmallows take the place of boring reading and math on these welcomed days, but not this year. The March winds came and went in February like little lambs who had lost their way, and there was no lion wind to be found stalking them.

The spring itself, once it commenced, could not hold itself back. Pussy willow and forsythia wands clamored for attention early on, and the crocuses poked their heads up on the same day the ground hog told us we would not have to wait six more weeks for spring this year. Then right on cue, the tulips and daffodils blossomed from dark green spikes, poking their way through the bare spots on the ground, causing riots of color where just days before there had been nothing but empty, brown patches of mud. At the same time, as if answering a special invitation, the seasonal birds returned to the area. After several early elopements, the happy couples made their nests in the usual places, and laid their eggs of bright blue, speckled gray, or muted whites.

Years ago, I read a memorable line from a very wise, unnamed author. It went something like this: "If I live to be 100, I will only have seen 100 springs." Those few words still resonate truth for me. The call for rebirth is faithfully renewed year after year, summoned by the Creator Himself. Though these days overflow with nature's endless treasures, their fragile beauty passes so quickly, I don't think I will ever get my fill of spring's exquisite gifts. This particular year had been no exception, nature's bounty got my attention along with thoughts of awe, and wide smiles of appreciation and praise.

Then without warning, our whole family became almost oblivious to the beauty outside. Something else, slower, grayer, and very sinister demanded our full attention. One of us had received a life-threatening diagnosis, something none of us had previously experienced.

My beloved sister, my newly suffering sibling, known to us all as the family health guru, was facing the biggest challenge of her life. She had been diagnosed with throat cancer, a sneaky coward of a disease that most often preys on the weak, the down and out, and the helpless. This time, the big "C" erroneously picked on someone at the peak of life, someone determined to fight each battle one by one, someone not accustomed to the word "surrender."

The battles commenced and fight she did, with no thought for herself. Those she loved, loved her back, and the family circled our wagons, so to speak. We all believed that she would be victorious; for her, there was no thought of any other option. My sister's growing faith helped strengthen her determined attitude; however, this was not sufficient to totally eliminate all of her pain, fear, or worry, during the long, uncomfortable days and nights she suffered. The rest of the family longed to build a deep protective moat around her, and to help her in any way we could to triumph over her relentless foe. At least one would have gladly changed places with her if he could do so, but most of the time we were left to watch from the sidelines, often feeling helpless as the toll on her health climbed day after day.

O God, I do not pretend to understand why terrible things happen to innocent people. However, I claim Your promise that You will be with my sister every step of the way. She has answered Your knock on her soul, and believes in Your Son.

As my sister continued her courageous fight back to a healthy life inside the house, the rest of the family simply ignored the pleasures of springtime beauty that continued happening outside without our permission. Enjoying a beautiful new world awakening with new life just did not seem right. There have been a few other times in my life when I remember not being able to justify why the sun continued to rise, the flowers bloomed, and the birds continued to sing, but each day they did just that. And this spring continued on with her performance, spinning and dancing to music we didn't want to hear.

My sister sought God's presence more and more, and her prayers were rising to Him day and night. By now we all knew my sister needed a miracle to claim victory over her foe, so we asked God for one, calling to Him to please come closer, to touch her, and heal her.

Unexpectedly, He brought us a diversion in the form of a little spotted tree frog with no previous claim to fame. In fact, this frog was so inconsequential a creature, at least to us, that he actually went unnamed by anyone for several weeks, even though observing him, as well as talking directly to him, became an anticipated, rare moment of pleasure in most of our days.

He was about the size of a golf-ball when his legs were pulled up beneath him, a dull, grayish-green color, decorated with irregular black splotches on his back. He had claimed, as if his own, the corner of an old square flowerpot at the end of the covered, white wooden front porch of my sister's home. Inside the square pot was a second, round pot filled with a rather scraggly, lifeless-looking plant that had survived the winter down in the basement. Perhaps no one had bothered to tell that plant that spring had come weeks ago. My sister still had hopes that the plant would become beautiful once again over the summer, nestled as it now was in the protected corner of the porch. As the days passed, and the plant received plenty of water and just enough sunlight, it slowly lived up to its potential, becoming a virtual haven for its resident frog. The newly resurrected plant eventually provided a continuous source of water, and attracted numerous bugs that often ended up either as savory treats, or full gourmet frog meals.

That little ordinary frog originally attracted, and then maintained our ongoing attention because of his one overt characteristic, his tenacious pot-clinging. He would hold on to the edge of his square pot for three or four days at a time, without even moving as far as we could tell. Then without any warning or a wave goodbye, he would disappear into a world only other frogs, worms, ants, and creatures like hobbits, could explore. We never saw him leave the pot, and we never saw how he returned, even though we checked on his status several times every day. We did think that jumping back up into that pot must have required a special type of frog-energy and a powerful pair of hind legs in so small a creature. We came to admire his accomplishments, such as they were.

As my sister's world became smaller due to the constraints of her illness, her front porch became a place of quiet retreat and frog watching. After weeks of observing this frog's amazing stamina in grasping the pot tightly for days on end, usually as he rested after returning from one of his frequent expeditions, my sister and brother-in-law finally gave him the name Clinger. After all, the desire "to cling," to just hold on to the side of his pot, took up most of his time and energy, and we all agreed the name was appropriate.

Sometimes, Clinger brought back friends he met on his travels, and invited them to share his summer home. Interestingly, they never overstayed their welcome, always leaving in a day or two. His return with guests always brought laughter and smiles to the people watching for him from inside the house, as well as a feeling of relief that Clinger was alive and well, and enjoying the company of others. His simple activities made our hearts feel a little lighter, and provided a much needed distraction from the darkness of illness that was overwhelming us much of the time. We found we could freely laugh at Clinger's antics without feeling any guilt.

Meanwhile, my sister was performing similar Clinger-like "holding-on" activities inside the house, as she continued to fight battles both big and small with her nemesis. When times got rough for her, and this happened often, given the weapons she was called upon to use, Clinger was a tiny model of persistence and encouragement. He had no idea how much he was impacting her and touching all others who had come to know about him and share his life vicariously.

O God, was the purpose of this little frog to pull us outside of the gray feeling that was inside my sister's house, into the bright shining rays of the sun, just beyond her front door? You continued to bless our family with the antics of this little fellow during these difficult times, and I know this was not a coincidence.

Meanwhile, the illness inside the house receded, and with it the dark, gray feeling faded away. The days lengthened into summer, a time my sister especially treasured with her family. With so many of them being teachers, they had long ago claimed their free summers for fun and togetherness. Gardening, swimming, camping, fishing and picnics filled their agendas. The air itself became lighter and brighter, and hopeful once again. My sister's cancer treatments were complete, and her strength was returning along with her appetite. There was to be a lull before any further testing would be done, so she chose this to live life fully, surrounded by her beloved family, each day being more precious to her than the last.

My sister reported Clinger's antics several times a week to interested family members, since there was no longer a need for us to make frequent visits to her house. Tales of Clinger's wandering ways gave us all a safe, lighthearted topic to utilize to keep our family in close touch. His return from one of his unknown destinations after being away for days at a time, always brought us together in short, phone-time celebrations of life's little victories, not to be missed even for a frog.

All through the heat of summer, Clinger came and went at will to his pot on the porch. No one ever did really see him do much of anything except cling to the side of that pot, then he would disappear. In fact, my sister got in the habit of touching him gently on his back every couple of days or so to assure herself that he was really still alive. Clinger did have a very satisfied smile on his face most of the time, his eyes closed to any and all distractions. By doing nothing but holding on and dreaming his dreams, he helped divert us from the more serious thing we had pushed down deep inside our very souls.

An unanticipated hurricane late in the summer caused the people living safely inside the house some concern for Clinger since he had been absent on one of his sabbaticals for several days. My brother-in-law finally found the missing adventurer secure and snug in the bottom of his pot, and promptly moved him into the garage for the storm's duration. When things were calm once again a couple of days later, Clinger and his pot were returned to his designated place in the porch corner. He was probably completely unaware that he had slept through one of the worst storms of the century.

Fall arrived full of spunk, and the leaves changed from a deep, lush green to those crisp gold, orange, and red colors that define the season's personality. Eventually, the leaves all turned brown and curled in on themselves, dropping to the ground, and requiring hours of attention to clear them away.

By now we were all wondering when Clinger would say goodbye and seek more protective shelter from the approaching winter weather. All the other frogs in the area had already vanished. The days were chilly, and the nights were downright cold. Quilts and blankets were now required on beds and recliners. It actually felt as though winter had already crossed our doorstep. Our early spring had been followed, as if by a special directive, by an early summer, then an early fall, and now an early winter.

On one visit to my sister's home, before I even rang the doorbell, I went to inspect the lonely porch pot to confirm for myself Clinger's habitation status. There was no frog holding onto the pot's edge. After going inside and performing the ritual familial greetings, I inquired about the last Clinger sighting. It had apparently been several days.

With my sister and me close on his heels, my brother-in-law sprinted outside to check on their little boarder, now considered a family mascot. Unable to see Clinger holding on to his usual spot, he pulled up the round inner pot with the plant that had now returned to its scraggly form once again. There miraculously, in an inch of water with ice around the edges was Clinger, stretched out full-length in the bottom of the square pot. We thought for sure he was dead once again, but as we watched, he slowly gathered his legs together and kicked himself to the side of the pot, underneath the top thin layer of ice. He had probably heard us talking about him and been rudely awakened from his nap.

"Unbelievable," my brother-in-law said. "Does he not know that it is way past time to find shelter for the winter? It is really cold out here. Soon the rest of the water in this pot will turn to solid ice and Clinger will not be able to move."

As this little frog's life story continued taking place outside on the porch, inside the house my sister's cancer was making itself felt strongly again. We all wanted to push the cancer away from her, to somehow hold it back. Medicine, surgery, or any treatment with a promise of helping were all bravely given a try. She fought valiantly once again, battle by battle, but she was getting very tired.

O God, I do not understand why we connect the fortitude of this little frog to live, to my sister's determination to live, but somehow we do. Their outcomes are already known to You, but are unknown to the rest of us. However, there is no doubt in my mind that You are in charge of them both, and for that I give You my continuous thanks.

So Clinger, with winter on his very doorstep, is still in his pot. One day soon we all know he will leave, and I doubt goodbyes to us will be high on his to-do list. He will finally be in a hurry to find a secure place to wait out the frigid season. We do not know where he will go, and we do not know for sure if he will come back. When he leaves, my sister will move his pot to her basement for the duration of the cold weather. She already has plans to put the pot with the scraggly plant back out on the porch when the pussy willow and the forsythia wands beckon her once again, in hopes that Clinger will come back in the new year to help her welcome the next spring.

O God, thank You for this little creature that helped us climb from the darkness that swallows lives, back into moments of light. While checking on Clinger day after day, we did not miss the beauty of Your spring, Your summer, or the extravagance of Your fall, and now winter. More than once, laughter abounded on that porch because of the tenacity of that little frog to just hold on. Take care of him this winter, just as I know, O God, You are taking care of my dear sister, each and every day.

Epilogue

That next year the escalating battles with cancer overwhelmed my sister and our family. Reports from the doctors brought word of my sister's failing health, and the ice inside of us all grew thicker. At times the rest of us felt so helpless, but like her little friend Clinger, my sister held on tight and refused to give up. We were all hoping and praying for a miracle of healing, but we did not witness this happening. My sister turned to God more and more, trusting Him to take charge as her strength waned, and the endless tests and radical surgery did nothing but steal more of the precious energy she needed to wrestle the cancer for life itself.

Spring again insistently followed the winter, even though once again such beauty didn't seem quite right to the people coming and going more and more frequently to my sister's house. The pot with the scraggly plant was returned to the porch, but as yet no Clinger had reported for duty.

One day, from her living room window, my sister watched her beloved grandchildren playing outside in her front yard, knowing well she was no longer able to join them in their games. She turned and looked deep into my eyes so like her own, and said to me, "There it is in front of me, the beautiful circle of life, that is what it is all about." She was calm, and had a quiet, gentle peace about her.

More rapidly now, despite the continued efforts of many doctors, and the endless loyal love and care of her husband, children, and her extended family, the cancer gained power. One beautiful day in late May, my precious sister, whom I had the privilege of knowing her entire life, went to sleep for the last time, her beloved husband near her side. She went to her heavenly home, where in time so quick it is beyond our comprehension, wholeness and peace and joy replaced all the agony and pain of the past months.

Many mourned her passing, and until her Celebration Life Service, most of our family had no idea of the numerous lives she had lovingly guided or touched over the last 66 years as a friend, a teacher and a coach. We said our public goodbyes out loud to others, but our private goodbyes will continue until we each meet her once again.

As for Clinger, that little frog did not return to his pot on the porch that summer. Perhaps he had gone ahead of my sister to that place called heaven which we can only imagine. He was a first-rate little frog with a definite aptitude for holding on to a pot. I can envision the Father greeting them both with open arms, and possibly saying with His wonderful smile:

"Well done, good and faithful servants. Well done, indeed."

THE END

IN MEMORY OF

GAY PETRLIK

1947-2013

By the time "Moon-Night Visitors," the last story written for our book together, was completed, my sister Gay was unable to draw the final illustration. The other stories each have an original chalk drawing made by her. We talked of keeping the picture page for "Moon-Night Visitors" the color black, since the narrative is about night-time happenings. I realized after she had died that the picture had to reflect Gay's freedom from disease and pain, and her transition to an infinite place filled with love, peace, and timelessness where she will be waiting when it is time for us to meet her again, a place where I can imagine her dancing.

Thus the distant beauty of light within the chosen night photograph: "Faraway Moon."

Until later then Dear Gay,

Love, Jenny.

ABOUT THE AUTHOR

This is S. Jenny Boyer's second book about the faith lessons she has learned from animals. She lives on an acre in the country where creature visitation is always a possibility. She and her husband are retired and treasure this time together. This book is a way for her to share with others her belief in God, and a way to remember her sister, Gay.

There is no creature,
regardless of its apparent insignificance,
that fails to show us something of God's goodness.
Thomas à Kempis

CPSIA information can be obtained at www.ICGtesting.com
Printed in the USA
BVOW10s2008091014

369946BV00003B/3/P

9 781612 443157